Dear Reader:

Solvay Pharmaceuticals, Inc. is pleased to present you with this complimentary copy of *Everything in Its Place: My Trials and Triumphs with OCD.*

Since being diagnosed with obsessive compulsive disorder, the author, Marc Summers, has devoted considerable time and energy to raising awareness about mental health and helping to reduce the stigma surrounding mental illness. He has inspired people suffering from OCD and other anxiety disorders to seek treatment. We applaud his courage in revealing his personal struggles with OCD, to help others better understand the nature of this illness.

Like Marc, Solvay Pharmaceuticals, Inc. is a committed partner in the mental health community. We will continue to help people with mental disorders through the development of state-of-the-art treatment options.

Solvay Pharmaceuticals commends Marc on his efforts. We hope you enjoy Marc's story, and take his message of hope and understanding with you.

Sincerely,
Steve Jennings
Director of Mental Health Marketing
Solvay Pharmaceuticals, Inc.

everything in its place

jeremy p. tarcher/putnam

a member of penguin putnam inc.

new york

everything in its place

my trials
and
triumphs
with
obsessive
compulsive
disorder

marc summers
with eric hollander, m.d.

Most Tarcher/Putnam books are available at special quantity discounts for bulk purchases for sales promotions, premiums, fund-raising, and educational needs. Special books or book excerpts also can be created to fit specific needs. For details, write Putnam Special Markets, 375 Hudson Street, New York, NY 10014.

Jeremy P. Tarcher/Putnam
a member of
Penguin Putnam Inc.
375 Hudson Street
New York, NY 10014
www.penguinputnam.com
First trade paperback edition 2000

The Library of Congress has cataloged the hardback
edition as follows:
Summers, Marc.
Everything in its place : my trials and triumphs with
obsessive compulsive disorder / Marc Summers with
Eric Hollander.
p.   cm.
ISBN 0-87477-990-1
1. Obsessive-compulsive disorder. Popular works. I. Hollander, Eric, date.   II. Title.
RC533.S86   1999   99-27534 CIP
616.85'227—dc21
ISBN 1-58542-108-1 (special markets edition)
Printed in the United States of America
1   3   5   7   9   10   8   6   4   2

This book is printed on acid-free paper. ∞

Book design by Amanda Dewey

acknowledgments

There have been many people along the way who have participated in this project. First of all, Kenneth Wapner and Jennifer
Wolfson, two of the most amazing people I have ever met. Their
intelligence and sensitivity are responsible for taking this project
from zero to sixty in record time.

Dr. Eric Hollander and Mariette Hartley who, by some stroke
of luck or fate or maybe the booking genius of Larry Ferber,
showed me the light and the path to getting rid of the silliness.

To the Kahn family, especially Darcie, Beatrice, and Marty,

and also Jake McDowell and his mom, Debbie, some of my first OCD friends. People like this definitely make the world a better place.

The people at Ketchum. They performed miracles in my life and, in turn, in the lives of others. A gigantic thank-you and a big hug to Colleen Brady and Hal Walker.

My new family at Porter Novelli, including Natalie Adler, Jeff Macdonald, Reisha Kelsey, and most especially to my travel buddy, Megan Pace. Megan and I do not necessarily agree on politics or sports, but her professionalism, dedication, and ability to go far beyond the call of duty at all times are to be applauded. Someday, she will definitely be that CEO in the corner office. See, I said it!

Mary Guardino, the most energetic woman I have ever met. Your sense of humor and your guidance mean more to me than you know. Tom Styron, the new man in charge, whose vision is inspirational. Trent Owen, for letting me share some time.

Fred Rothenberg at NBC News, who said all along it was the right thing to do. You were correct, and it helped many more with the visits to Matt Lauer and Oprah Winfrey. And to Sara James, the first person allowed to really mess up the place. You did good and thanks. To John Hannah at *People* magazine who jump-started all the media.

Mr. Steve Jennings, the hardest-working man in the business and one of the nicest. I value our friendship and will miss working with you. Good luck on the new gig. David Dodd for his wisdom and leadership. And to a very special lady, Janice McClure. Everyone should have a friend like you.

Wendy Hubbert, who understood the mission immediately and is a major supporter in so many ways. You always bring me good news. To Lori Fuller, you helped get it over the top.

Mark Reiter, a friend since the '80s who always stuck by me, pushed me, believed in my talent, and never gave up. It took over ten years, but we finally got a book! And thanks for almost always returning my phone calls! This would never have happened without you.

Richard Lawrence. If you look up "friend" in the dictionary, it is your picture that is the model. Thanks for absolutely everything.

My parents Martin and Lois and my sister Lori, who have a sense of humor about it and continue to try and understand this thing that has been handed down. Thanks for the support. To my brother Mike, the voice of reason, who dealt with this from the other side. And Clara Essak, Bobba, thanks for teaching me the wax paper trick, for letting me watch you sweep the street, and for providing me with all the summers of fun.

Burt, Lynn, Ali, and Liza Dubrow, for listening, understanding, and sharing the laughs. Mark Smith, a man who has been there from the beginning and shared the good times and the not so good. My other "sister," Merrie Dudley, who for the past eight years has somehow been involved in my professional life, even if it was just to take one of those phone calls at 2 A.M.!

A big thanks to Diane Considine, Vernal Cripe, Harold Hartman, and Chet Kubit for laying the foundation.

To Alice, Matthew, and Meredith, who know it has not always been easy to live with the guy who followed them and everyone else around the house, touched walls, and often made no sense. I love you all very much and appreciate your patience.

And for everyone else I forgot to mention, Thanks . . . especially Harvey for letting me vent. And last but certainly not least, Windex and Reggie. Who knew animals could be so much fun?

To Alice, Matthew,
and Meredith

*Because of your
love, patience,
and understanding,
I was able
to move forward.*

contents

foreword by eric hollander

I first met Marc Summers on his television talk show, *Biggers and Summers*. As a leading expert on obsessive compulsive disorder, I had become involved with the Obsessive Compulsive Foundation in a public campaign to increase awareness of OCD. I had been booked on radio and television programs as part of this public education campaign, and before I was due to go on Marc's show, he took me aside. "I've been up all night," he said in a shaky voice. "I was pacing back and forth, wondering whether I should talk to you. I think I have OCD."

I asked him a series of simple screening questions: do you

need things to be even, symmetrical, or "just so"; do you have to check over and over if the door is locked, if the oven is still on, or whether you've run someone over with your car; do you experience disturbing, repetitive thoughts that you can't resist, such as fear that people close to you will be harmed; do you worry about dirt, germs, or contamination; do you wash or shower excessively; do you have trouble throwing things away, such as newspapers or lists; do you have counting rituals, or touching or tapping habits?

When Marc answered affirmatively to many of these questions, I told him that he might, indeed, have obsessive compulsive disorder. We had to break to prepare for the show, so I gave him my card and told him if he wanted to talk further, I was available. Then we were hustled on stage. A microphone was clipped to my jacket's lapel, and the stage hand counted down ten, nine, eight . . . and then were on the air. The excitement of live television was a real change of pace for me, since I spend most of my time in hospital outpatient clinics, in research laboratories, or hunkered down in university libraries.

In the back of my mind, though, I was thinking that the obvious reluctance Marc felt to tell me, a doctor, in private, of his suspicion that he had OCD indicated that he was nowhere near ready to admit to the world that he might have the disorder. So imagine my surprise when Marc admitted to having obsessive compulsive symptoms right at the beginning of the show.

It was an incredibly brave thing to do, and I felt a surge of gratitude to Marc. He was doing for obsessive compulsive disorder what Magic Johnson did for HIV, Mary Tyler Moore did for diabetes, and Naomi Judd did for hepatitis. Whenever a celebrity comes forth and talks on television about his or her struggle with an illness, there usually is a huge response from people who have been suffering in silence, suspecting something was wrong with them but most of the time not knowing what it was or how to find out more about it. In a survey of 701 members of the Obsessive Compulsive Foundation, I found that approximately 25 percent of obsessive compulsive sufferers first seek treatment after seeing a report in the media about OCD. The first step in increasing recognition of OCD, which leads to effective treatment, is to get the word out. And the most effective way to do that is to have someone like Marc—who has a great sense of humor, who's bright, who people can identify with—humanize the disorder.

With the cameras rolling, Marc leaned over, a sheen of guilt and apprehension on his face. His voice came in a low revealing rush as he told his television audience about his neatness compulsions. I saw in him a truly outstanding spokesperson for the disorder—someone who could play an important role in educating the public and encouraging people to come forward and seek help.

OCD is a disorder that has desperately needed a spokesperson. It has long had a stigma attached to it. The Catholic Church in the Middle Ages attributed its symptoms to the devil. Shakespeare used Lady Macbeth and her compulsive handwashing ("Out, damn spot! out, I say!") to signify obsessional madness. In Victorian times, people with OCD provided the classic definition of insanity. And even recently, OCD has been significantly misunderstood. Freud wrote a landmark study of an obsessive compulsive patient he dubbed the Rat Man, a young man who was plagued by intrusive and repetitive thoughts that rats were going to eat him and his father. Freud, typically, attributed Rat Man's symptoms to problems with toilet training, and for most of this century that diagnosis held: the disorder was commonly believed to be a psychologically based problem, caused by early childhood conflicts, and treated with psychoanalysis.

Since psychoanalysis has proved to be ineffective in treating the disorder, the consensus in the medical community through the early 1980s was that OCD was not responsive to treatment. And the prevalence of the illness was grossly underestimated. It's only in the past 15 years or so that we have realized that OCD is a medical disorder, having to do with an imbalance of neurotransmitters in the brain, which we now estimate affects roughly six million Americans—none of whom are crazy or possessed by the devil. Happily, in the last 15 years, doctors and scientists have made important discoveries about OCD and its treatment. We can now effectively treat the disorder with medication and behavior therapy, and we have a startlingly high success rate. Seventy percent of OCD sufferers who undergo treatment report a substantial improvement in their symptoms and their quality of life.

But even with all these advances, there are still millions of OCD sufferers who don't know that they have a disorder or are afraid to seek treatment because of the stigma attached to OCD. One of the things I always wished I had to give these people is a story like Marc's. It's the story of a guy who was able to face OCD head-on and overcome it. Marc is living proof that there's no reason a stigma should be attached to the disorder.

I first became interested in studying OCD when I was a resident in psychiatry at Mt. Sinai Hospital in New York City, doing research on schizophrenia and Alzheimer's disease. While the science was fascinating, because these are disorders that didn't usually respond to treatment, working with these patient populations was tough. When I started reading the emerging literature on OCD, I realized that this was another common brain-based disorder, but one that might respond to treatment better than Alzheimer's or schizophrenia. A particular neurotransmitter, a chemical used to send messages between brain cells, had been implicated in OCD, and this neurotransmitter, serotonin, was known to be affected by drug therapy.

In 1986, I began to research the neurobiology and psychopharmacology of OCD. Nineteen eighty-six turned out to be a watershed year. Studies were initiated at 20 sites across the country to test Anafranil (clomipramine), a medication that in the past had been used to treat depression, on people with OCD. The studies were sponsored by the pharmaceutical industry to determine for the Food and Drug Administration whether this medication was a safe and effective treatment for OCD.

I was involved in a number of medication trials that took place at the Columbia University's New State Psychiatric Institute. We advertised on radio, television, and in *The New York Times* and *Daily News*, to find subjects to test new medications for OCD. The ads ran: "Do you have disturbing thoughts that you can't get out of your head? Do you wash your hands over and over? Do you need everything to be perfect?" We were overwhelmed by the response, and found ourselves inundated by people wanting to participate in the study. It was a strong signal that the number of people who had the disorder had been grossly underestimated.

The second thing that completely changed the minds of the Columbia researchers was the dramatic improvement we saw in the symptoms of 70 percent of the OCD sufferers that we treated with Anafranil. This result exploded the theory that OCD was psychologically rather than physically based, and completely changed the way the medical community viewed and treated OCD.

Successive trials showed that other drugs, called selective serotonin reuptake inhibitors (SSRIs), such as Luvox (fluvoxamine), Prozac (fluoxetine), Paxil (paroxetine), and Zoloft (sertraline) were just as effective as Anafranil in treating OCD but were better tolerated by patients.

This was an incredibly exciting time for me. I had found my life's work. I continued to do research on the neurobiology of OCD, and I started evaluating and treating people with the disorder. As I listened to their stories, I realized that many of these patients were suffering from other disorders along with OCD. This led to my discovery of the "OCD spectrum," a group of disorders which I believe to be closely related to OCD.

This OCD spectrum includes: body dysmorphic disorder (people obsessed with imagined bodily imperfections); eating disorders, such as anorexia nervosa; hypochondriasis (people obsessed with imagined physical illness); Sydenham's chorea (a rare disorder that follows a strep throat infection characterized by involuntary movements); autism; and Tourette's syndrome (characterized by elaborate motor and vocal tics: eye blinking, humming, and shouting profanity, for instance). We found that 50 to 90 percent of people with Tourette's, for example, also have

OCD symptoms, and 10 percent of people with OCD also have Tourette's.

I also began to study a whole series of impulsive disorders that involve repetitive behaviors and are driven by pleasure seeking and arousal gratification, such as pathological gambling, trichotillomania (pulling out one's own hair over and over), compulsive shopping, and compulsive sexual disorders. I found that the same medications that worked on people with OCD also worked on people with OCD spectrum disorders.

In 1993, my colleagues (Drs. Concetta DeCaria, Dan Stein, Daphne Simeon, Bonnie Aronowitz, and Lisa Cohen) and I moved back to Mt. Sinai and initiated the Compulsive, Impulsive, and Anxiety Disorders Program, which I currently direct. Our research focuses on the study of neurotransmitter and neuropeptide function, neuropsychiatric function, brain imaging by Positron Emission Tomography (PET) scans, assessing the impact of OCD on quality of life, and developing new treatments for unresponsive patients.

Unfortunately, there is still much that is not known about the causes of OCD and why some patients don't respond to treatment. To address these unanswered questions, I have organized the International OCD Conferences, which meet on an annual basis in Europe and North America. These conferences bring together the world's experts on OCD in small closed workshops to reach a consensus about the direction of future OCD research. I have also helped organize the International OCD Consortium, a cooperative of research groups around the world that work together to address the needs of OCD patients.

Doctors report that some OCD patients, up to 30 percent, don't respond well to medication. Many of these patients have subtle neurological "soft signs": problems with fine motor coordination, frequent facial grimacing, difficulty drawing a three-dimensional cube, and difficulties reading a map. These soft signs are a reflection of altered brain circuitry in OCD patients. The more severe the soft signs, the more severe the obsessions. Soft signs may be a way of predicting lack of response to serotonin-based OCD medications. Non-responders seem to differ in terms of their serotonin function and the activity level of certain brain regions, as measured by PET scans. Fortunately, a portion of these patients may respond to medications other than SSRIs.

I find my patients to be engaging, intelligent people who have good insight into their condition and a real will to get better. In helping them, I focus on finding what would motivate them to get better, something in their life that they really want to do but that OCD is preventing them from doing. One of my patients underwent a major breakthrough when she realized she wanted to be more involved with her kids. I've seen other patients who were motivated to get better when they saw how the disorder was interfering with an important relationship. This was the case with Jack Nicholson's character in the movie *As Good As It Gets*: he wanted the girl, and she made it clear that in order to get her, he would have to get better, or become "a better man," as he says in the film. As you'll read in the following pages, Marc Summers was moved to begin therapy when he hit rock bottom and realized the disorder was hurting his relationship with his wife and kids.

Some of my patients with OCD are high functioning like Marc, while others are more disabled. But the good news is that most respond well to treatment, and it's been very gratifying for me to help them get better. It takes tremendous courage for my patients to admit they have a problem and to seek out help. It also takes courage for them to overcome anxieties and face their fears, and to find the motivation to follow through with their treatment.

Marc has written a book for everyone with OCD, their families and their friends and loved ones. It's the book we've all been waiting for, a book that will entertain, inspire, and enlighten. As a doctor working in the field, I know that the biggest barriers to treating OCD are denial and silence. My deepest hope is that Marc's positive story will galvanize people suffering in silence to finally seek and receive appropriate and effective help.

introduction

From the time I was six years old, everything in my world had to be perfect. My clothes had to be folded a certain way. The shirts hanging in my closet had to be a quarter-inch apart, no more, no less, with all the hangers facing the same direction. My books were organized alphabetically and lined up so that they were exactly the same distance from the lip of the shelf. I shined my shoes each day until they glowed and I could see my face in them. If I erased something on a homework paper and left the slightest smudge or, God forbid, a hole, I'd redo the assignment on a fresh sheet of paper because I thought my failure to do so would result in something bad happening to me or to my parents. One of us would have a freak accident or contract a deadly disease. I thought I was the only kid in the world who felt this way. I thought I was crazy, so I kept the secret of my bizarre behaviors locked deep inside.

I was an odd kid, and not only because of my fanatical neatness and strange, fearful thoughts. I was odd because hosting television shows was all I ever dreamt about. I would come home from Miss Helms' kindergarten class and tune in to *Art Linkletter's House Party*. On each episode, Art talked to four kids about life. Unlike all my friends, I wanted to be Art, not the kids being interviewed! I can tell you who produced and announced programs that went off the air 40 years ago because as soon as I could read I was studying the credits on every TV show.

I had no idea I had obsessive compulsive disorder (OCD) when I was a child. In fact, I only learned about OCD a few short years ago. As a child and until my diagnosis in 1996, I didn't relate my fanatical neatness to my drive to be a TV personality. But looking back, those two parts of my personality were tightly entwined. At age six, I was driven, focused: I was determined that my room be spotless and my closet organized like a drill sergeant's; and I was just as determined to be on TV.

Either by luck or determination, my dreams came true. Those of you who discovered me as the host of a messy television program called *Double Dare* probably had no idea I was suffering from OCD. At that point, neither did I! All I knew was that I hated the part of my job that involved getting dumped in vats of goo or smeared with slime. On the air, I always laughed good-naturedly when I was slimed, but inside I was squirming.

Double Dare was *Jeopardy!* meets *Beat the Clock*. The kids who came on the show had to answer a question on history, geography, or pop culture. If they failed to answer the question correctly, they had to take on a physical challenge that usually involved being splattered with green liquid or some other disgusting concoction. The show's producers were ingenious in devising new ways for the contestants—and me—to become filthy. The kids loved seeing their adult host covered in gunk, and so we were doused, dunked, splattered, smeared, and slimed with oatmeal, applesauce, raw eggs, vanilla pudding, and chocolate syrup. Kids belly-flopped into a four-thousand-gallon tub filled with cold baked beans. It was truly repulsive. The most disgusting stunt the producers invented involved dog food. Competing teams of ten-year-olds with catapults on either end of the side stage heaved huge gobs of moist Alpo at each other. The sight of flying dog food and the smell that pervaded the studio that day sent me careening off stage, gagging.

As soon as the camera stopped on *Double Dare*, the instant we were off the air, I'd rip off my jacket, shirt, and tie, standing naked from the waist up in front of 300 eight- to eleven-year-olds. The producers hated this, but I couldn't help myself. I couldn't stand still with all that messy stuff on me. I took long hot showers, first in the studio and then at home.

After these showers I was generally fine until I'd scratch my ear and pull out a piece of green slime, or until the whipped cream that had been shoved in my face and had gone up my nostrils began to ferment, filling my head with the smell of sour milk. I'd have to practically snort cologne to mask that odor.

I'll never forget the smell of the Philadelphia television studio in which we first shot *Double Dare*, WHYY, a PBS station across from Independence Mall. The cleaning crew did a noble job of swabbing the place down after each show. But the food wormed its way into all the sets, into every crack in the walls, floor, and ceiling. The place smelled like a refrigerator where the food had been left to rot—a cruddy, putrid smell. One day the studio cleanup crew all broke out in skin rashes—that's how gross it was. Though I didn't know it at the time, it was exponentially grosser for me because it dovetailed with my obsessive need for cleanliness.

I left *Double Dare* in 1994 to do adult television, moving to New York City, where I co-hosted *Biggers and Summers,* a talk show on the Lifetime cable network. It was there, finally, at the age of 43 that I realized I had obsessive compulsive disorder. It happened by a fluke: we were doing a show to raise the public's awareness of OCD, and while scanning my prep material the night before, I realized I had the disorder. I actually "outed" myself on the air.

From the moment I went public with my OCD, my life changed. It was over a year before I sought treatment and began to get better, but I immediately understood that the bizarre behaviors that had made me different from other kids were caused by a chemical imbalance in my brain. I thought and acted the way I did because my brain had hiccups, as my doctor liked to say. The disorder was something I was born with, like the color of my eyes.

Now I work closely with the OC Foundation, going across the country, talking about OCD. Although it can be a grave and difficult condition, I like to inject a little levity into a disorder that was thought to have been spawned by the devil in the Middle Ages and that defined madness in Victorian times.

OCD affects roughly six million Americans. This book will give you a good understanding of the causes and treatments of OCD, but it's not meant to be a detailed clinical examination of the disorder's pathology, neurochemistry, or treatment process. Instead, it charts my sometimes harrowing, often humorous, and ultimately inspiring personal journey from compulsive room cleaner to family man, TV personality, and national spokesperson for the disorder. I want to clear up myths and misinformation and wipe out the bad vibes that have long surrounded OCD.

For those of you who suspect you have the disorder, I hope you will gain confidence from my story and learn to see the positive side of living with OCD. Frankly, I think almost everyone has a touch of the disorder, and we can learn to channel it in productive ways. It could be that the fast-track CEO in the corner office you know, the one who's always on time, who's on top of every detail and can find every piece of paper in her neat desk, is an example of someone who's learned to live successfully with OCD. If you suspect you have the disorder or know someone who does, I hope this book will help you realize the difference between superstition, caution, and true obsessive compulsive behavior, and help you understand a little more clearly what's going on inside the head of someone with OCD.

Enjoy my story, and, by the way, try not to bend the pages while you're reading. I'M JUST KIDDING!!!

Be well.

Marc Summers

| *one* |

the public face and
the private torment

On October 18, 1994, I was finally going on *The Tonight Show,*
where one appearance can make or break a career. Appearing on
The Tonight Show would fulfill one of my lifelong dreams. Johnny
Carson had been my idol as a child. Other kids had posters of
Mickey Mantle or the Beatles on the wall, but not me. I had
Johnny Carson. But by the time I made it to the show, Johnny was
gone. Jay Leno ruled the big desk.

I knew Jay from way back. When I started doing bits at the
Comedy Store on Sunset Boulevard in Los Angeles there were
three guys you could tell were going to be stars: Robin Williams,

David Letterman, and Jay Leno. Jay was a journeyman comic—
he'd go out on the road, work anywhere. Big clubs, little clubs.
He was always working, and he is still one of the hardest-working
men in show business. Johnny took thirteen weeks off each year;
Jay takes two. He also has the reputation for treating guests like
human beings even if they're not as successful as he is, which is
more than you can say for most people in L.A.

After 25 years on television, I had finally cracked into that
dubious elite where—gulp—people will pick up the phone and
get back to you. My agents had been trying to book me on *The
Tonight Show* for years. Then, suddenly, Leno's talent coordinator, Mike Alexander, called to schedule me for an appearance to
talk about *Double Dare* and promote my new shows, *What Would
You Do?* and *Our Home.*

I was booked, bounced, and rebooked nine times. Late-night
talk show talent coordinators have a difficult job. Agents and
publicists call them constantly, trying to get their clients an appearance. A show will always lead with the biggest star and book
smaller fry that it thinks will get along with him or her. So, for
whatever reason—the producers didn't like the mix of guests a
particular week, or whatever—they'd book me, I'd get all excited
that "next week it was going to happen!" and then they'd call a
week, or even a day, before my scheduled appearance and cancel me. Sometimes they'd call and say, "We rescheduled your
appearance but we don't know for when." This went on for almost a year. I'd heard horror stories of people who were booked
for as long as three years and never ended up doing the show
at all.

It was nerve-wracking, especially for someone like me with

obsessive compulsive disorder. I didn't know the root cause, but I did know that being bounced time and again off *The Tonight Show* was making me nuts. Lack of punctuality and order awakened in me then—and sometimes still does now—strong emotional responses, from intense anxiety to anger. I was also aware that I had secret rituals, magic incantations and spells that I used to ensure that disaster didn't strike. I needed, for example, to read the back of the cereal box at breakfast over and over with complete fluidity or, I was convinced, the flight that I had booked for later that week would crash. I kid you not, I believed (as do millions of other Americans with OCD) that my well-being hinged on such absurdities.

Alexander and Leno wanted Marc Summers the magician, which was the way I had begun my career in show business, back in Indianapolis, where, as a teenager, I made rabbits pop out of hats at birthday parties.

"Do some magic with Jay," Mike said. "That will work well for your segment."

My segment was six minutes of the show wedged between commercials. It could catapult me to a new level of "visibility," as they say in the industry.

I had worked long and hard to get away from being billed as a magician. I was a television host, a teen icon, a comic. To focus my appearance on doing tricks made me shudder. What was I, a dancing poodle?

Finally, Mike Alexander gave me an ultimatum: if you want to do the show, you do a trick.

In this business you learn to please people, or you die trying. I'd do a trick.

If I was going to do a trick, I wanted it to be a card trick. No dice, they said. Jay wouldn't be sufficiently involved if I did a card trick. I called my friend Stan, a master magician. "Cut and restore Jay's tie," he suggested.

Jay's guys loved it.

What had I gotten myself into? I was going to do a trick I'd never performed before on the single most important television appearance of my life. I practiced and practiced my trick. Then I was bumped, and bumped again.

The tenth booking was the charm, or so it seemed. The show sent a limo to pick me up, but it arrived late. That was particularly unsettling since I was ready—as I always am—an hour early. I had laid out my suit, tie, shirt, and socks the night before. My magic props were in their little black cloth bag. I'd polished and brushed my shoes.

I paced the house. I lived with my family in a gated community, so I had to wait for security to telephone the limo's arrival. God, I thought, as I waited and waited, this is how they're going to tell me they bumped me again. They're just not going to pick me up. I would learn later that stress brought out my OCD symptoms, one of which was repetitive thoughts. At the time, I thought it was perfectly natural that my mind was on a loop, endlessly repeating the cut-and-restore tie trick.

Finally, the phone rang. The limo had arrived. It turned out that the driver had gotten lost.

I was in a state of acute anxiety as we whizzed down the Ventura Freeway—it was only a 20- or 30-minute drive to the studio from my house. I tried to make conversation with the driver—anything was better than being inside my head, replaying *ad nauseam* the tie routine. Suddenly, I felt a sickeningly familiar thud-thud thud-thud.

I leaned forward. "Is everything OK?"

"Sir, it seems we have a flat tire."

Had the show done it intentionally? Was this a premeditated break-down designed to strand undesired guests on the freeway? I couldn't believe it. God, I thought, is not pleased with me today. What else could go wrong?

The driver called the automobile club. I climbed from the car and started pacing along the shoulder of the Ventura Freeway. Auto clubs are the same the world over: sometimes technicians can arrive in 10 minutes; sometimes they take two hours. I kept checking my watch; it was a quarter to four, and the show started taping at 5:30. We were 15 minutes from the studio, near White Oak Avenue, and I was tempted to grab my suit and stick my thumb in the air.

AAA arrived. I stood in the swirling exhaust, cars whipping past, staring at the two guys who scrambled to change the flat on the big black limo.

When we finally arrived in Burbank, I arranged my belongings, as I always do before shows, in my small dressing room. I must have been nervous, because my OC symptoms were strong. I took my suit from its plastic dry-cleaning bag (I always put a plastic bag around a suit before putting it in an overnight bag) and hung it in the wardrobe closet, maniacally smoothing its nonexistent wrinkles and picking microscopic specks of lint from its crisp shoulders and lapels. I folded and refolded the plastic bag, placing it on the dressing-room couch in the middle of the right-side cushion, moving the bag around for several minutes until it was precisely centered. I could have been hanging a painting in the Louvre. I put my magic props on the vanity table, arranging and rearranging them until they sat at perfect angles to each other.

Jay came in, startling me. "Sorry you got bumped so many times," he said.

"I'm glad I'm finally here!" I replied.

We reminisced briefly about our Comedy Store days, and then I went to makeup. It was a thrill to be sitting in the same makeup room that Johnny Carson had used. *The Tonight Show* is one of the original, anchor shows of TV. It's living history. And I was a part of it.

I went back to my dressing room and put on my Joseph Abboud suit. This suit was my pride and joy, ridiculously expensive, with a subtle check design. I only wore it for special show biz occasions—like my first appearance on *The Tonight Show.*

Jay's audio man came in and clipped a microphone onto my lapel. Someone went over the questions Jay would ask and the responses I would give. (They pre-interview guests long before the actual show, but they go over the information again before taping to prevent guests from freezing up.) My mouth was parched. I was drinking gallons of water, but all it seemed to do was make me run to the bathroom every twenty seconds. My agent, Richard Lawrence, and my publicist, Coleen Gunderson, came in to lend support. But I was too nervous to carry on a conversation.

While waiting for my segment, we watched the show on the dressing-room monitor. The night before, Jay had made a nasty comment about Burt Reynolds' less-than-pretty divorce from Loni Anderson. Tonight, Burt was guesting on the show, and he was mad. We've all seen *Deliverance,* so we know Burt is capable of some odd behavior. But the night of this particular show, he was in an especially weird, vindictive mood. He said, in reference to Jay's nasty comment, "That was a cutting remark, so I'm going to even the score," and he brought out a pair of scissors and cut Jay's tie in half.

Out in the hall I heard a flurry of running feet. "Burt cut Jay's tie!" several people said. Leno's staff was in an uproar.

I sat there with my mouth hanging open. *Oh no,* I thought. *Now what do I do? Jay doesn't have a tie! What am I going to do my trick with?* I had an overwhelming urge to hail a cab (with well-inflated tires) and go home.

But it had been a long road to *The Tonight Show.* I had rechecked my props ten thousand times in preparation. I was staying. I was relieved to see Jay return from the commercial break with a new tie.

An angry, weirded-out Burt Reynolds makes good television, so Jay and his producers stuck with him. Instead of doing the usual star segment through two commercial breaks, Burt did three. The tone of the show was combative, confrontational. Burt was sullen, swaggering, sarcastic, and aggressive. It was a battle of testosterone. Jay kept pummeling Burt, making references to the size of Loni's divorce settlement, making fun of Burt's being on a book tour for his autobiography, a book he hadn't actually written. Soon, Burt was on his knees. Jay wouldn't give in, which is not Jay's reputation—he's known as a nice guy. But Burt, in the kind of nasty supercilious mood he was in, brings out the worst in people.

Right before the third commercial break, after which I was

due to go on, Jay closed in for the *coup de grace*. He opened the book to a 1972 *Cosmopolitan* magazine photo of Burt naked. Burt recalled his embarrassment as the photo editors had peered over the print of the photograph with magnifying glasses, inspecting his body.

"They needed magnifying glasses?" Jay said, referring to the size of Burt's manhood.

The audience erupted. Burt had been set up, he knew it, and he was livid as the show went to commercial.

Jay had time for only one more guest, but there were two of us scheduled.

Chaos erupted in the hall. "Summers or Carrot Top? Summers or Carrot Top?" Leno's staff shouted. This was every performer's nightmare: me versus the then-biggest comedian on college campuses. To my horror, the consensus among the show staff was that Carrot Top had bigger mojo than Summers.

My publicist and agent came into my dressing room and said, "You may not get on tonight."

"Let's go with Carrot Top," said a Leno executive.

My publicist stepped into the hall. "This is enough already," she said. "You've canceled us nine times. You can run Carrot Top tomorrow. Put Marc on tonight."

It was incredible: Leno's staff saw things our way.

From there, everything was a blur. The stage manager told me to stand by the stage entrance and watch the monitor. When *The Tonight Show* insignia came on, the band would stop playing and I'd hear my name.

"Dear God, please let me get through this and not embarrass myself!" I prayed.

". . . Marc Summers!" was the next thing I heard. It was one of the most frightening moments of my life. I walked onstage, the audience from the corner of my eye appearing in what we call in film a slow-motion swish-pan blur. They were clapping, but I could feel their rhythm, skittish and on edge, as they were waiting, with a quickened sense of anticipation and embarrassment, to see what new humiliations would ensue. As a performer, you can't really see an audience, so you learn to have an aural sense of them. I angled toward Jay, propelled across the stage by instinct, shaking his hand and sitting down in the chair next to the big desk in one fluid motion.

I knew I was walking into the lion's den. Two titans of show business were going head to head. And I knew both of them were thinking as I sat down, who the hell is Marc Summers? I had six minutes to prove myself; I needed to score. It's a one-shot deal out there. There are no retakes, no second chances. I wasn't nervous; I was petrified. I began to banter with Jay, as all guests do. I felt Jay relax a little: he had been sparring with one of the all-time champs. I sensed he had no idea why I was on the show. And neither had I. I was sitting up there purely because of the superb work of my publicist.

Now, let's get one thing straight. I have no illusions about my status in the Hollywood food chain. I'm still best known for my long stint on *Double Dare*. My weekly adventures of being submerged in a vat of applesauce, or dragged through oatmeal or green goo, make good conversation fodder. Jay, with a nervous eye on Burt, jumped on my role in *Double Dare*.

"Now, do you like doing the messy stuff especially?" he asked.

This wasn't a question we'd rehearsed, but Jay's allowed to ask whatever he wants.

Do I give the pat Nickelodeon-type response? *It's great! At least once a week, I know I'll get dessert before dinner.*

No, I thought. Don't be pat. You made it to the couch. Give a thoughtful, genuine answer.

"No, it's very strange," I said. "I'm Felix Unger: I'm a neatness fanatic, so it's weird that for the last nine years I've been doing that kind of TV."

A neatness fanatic, I thought. That's interesting. First time I had ever mentioned that. Why was I saying it now in front of a national TV audience?

In fact, this was the first time I had acknowledged—in my own mind—that spending hours and hours and more hours putting everything exactly the way it should be wasn't normal. I'd spent almost four decades obsessed with cleanliness, neatness, order, spaces, angles, borders, and straight lines. Everything I touched had to be spaced with exact precision. To me, that was being a "neat freak."

I had said it. I wasn't ashamed of it. In a world full of Oscar Madisons, you need a few Felix Ungers to balance things, right? Call me Felix.

I continued, "We've done some weird things on the show. We once built a container with 4,000 pounds of baked beans and made kids dive into it, which was really great."

"Gee," interjected Burt, "I wish I'd seen that." The audience laughed. Jay laughed. I laughed. Burt was deadpan.

Jay tried to pull us back on track. "You force kids' heads under baked beans?"

More laughter. I explained, smiling, "We have an obstacle course, and . . ."

Burt jumped in, cutting me off mid-sentence: "Who told you you were a neatness freak?"

Alarm clock. Needle scratch. Wrong answer buzzer.

"I just say that," Burt said with annoyance, "because your back is to me and I was just talking to a back."

I guess he thought it was the Burt Reynolds Show. Why should they bring anyone else out? At the time, Jay was still pretty green as *The Tonight Show* host. He'd been at it only about a year. On the other hand, Burt had been on *The Tonight Show* fifty times with Johnny Carson, and a few more with Jay. Burt Reynolds was the most veteran man on the stage that night, a fact he seemed eager to exploit.

I wanted to keep the peace. "No, no, I can talk to you, too, Burt."

"Watch out," Jay cautioned, "he's got scissors."

Burt hammered away, the scorn in his voice palpable. "I was just wondering, who told you you were neat?"

This was one angry guy. *Burt hates me*, I thought. *It's obvious.* I'm looking at this guy with a toupee and jeans that had been worn at least a hundred times and boots with a three-inch lift. Every morning he wakes up and has to transform himself into Burt Reynolds. I suddenly felt a wave of pity for the guy. In my mind I looked younger, dressed better, and was funnier. I tried to give him a quick non-answer grin, and go on with my segment. No dice.

"Who told you that you were a neatness fanatic?!" Burt repeated.

"My wife tells me that often," I said. "And," I patted his shoulder, "by the way, *I'm still married.*"

The audience went crazy. I glanced at Jay triumphantly. Jay jumped to his feet, eyes wide, and reached out to grab my arm. But it was too late. Burt dumped a mug of water into my crotch. I grabbed Jay's mug and tried to toss it on Burt, but Burt straight-armed me, bashing the mug into my mouth.

This is great, I thought. I'm finally on *The Tonight Show* and I'm engaging in fisticuffs with Burt Reynolds. It was, without a doubt, the most bizarre moment of my life. I was drenched, but I didn't even notice. At any other time, my normal obsession with my appearance would have made me acutely uncomfortable. I can't stand to have a hair out of place, the slightest spot or defect in my clothing. And here I was, sopping wet, my best suit blotched and spotted, my carefully coiffed hair hanging lankly over my forehead. But I was beyond concern for my appearance or comfort. I was trying to stay alive.

The audience roared. "You're not a neatness freak anymore," Burt scoffed.

I thought I'd lost a tooth; I was sure there was blood running down my face. I looked at Jay. He nodded comfortingly, which I took to mean—you're okay, you're blood-free.

"This is what's known as losing control of the program, ladies and gentlemen," Jay said. I think he felt a little protective of me. Yet he knew how good it was for the show.

I turned to the audience. "Burt Reynolds just dumped water on me. Did you notice that, folks?"

"And you'll treasure it later," Burt said, patting my hand.

"Don't touch me," I spat.

More laughter. Maybe I could still make this work. Maybe we could get along. I turned to Burt. "I used to be on your show all the time, *Win, Lose or Draw.* I loved that show."

"Funny," he shrugged, "I don't remember you."

"Oooooooh," said the audience.

So much for peace, love, and understanding. I turned back to Jay. "So, anyway, we were talking about being a neatness fanatic."

"Yeah," said Jay. "You started out as a magician, if I'm not mistaken."

Burt cackled like a hyena, laughing because the staff had tossed me a towel. He was sprawled on his chair, like he was soaking up rays at the beach. I couldn't resist. I blind-sided him with a mug of water, dousing him. The audience screamed in delight. Out of the corner of my eye, I could see folks in the balcony leap from their chairs to give me a standing ovation.

I learned later that my agent Richard was trying to stop the show. "My client looks like an idiot," he had said to the producers. "Stop taping!"

But my dignity, or career for that matter, was way down on the producers' list of priorities. They were looking for notoriety, ratings, hits in the press, and they knew they were going to get them.

Jay turned to his crew, appealing for a diplomatic solution. Before the show, Jay's producers had wanted to do a pie fight, but Jay had said no. Now, however, he mouthed to his crew, "Let's do the PIE."

Burt and I were drying ourselves off.

"It's all right," Burt said, "I deserved that."

"You deserved it?" I asked, quizzically.

"I deserved it. As I was saying to your wife the other night . . ."

Another wave of laughter. This would never end.

"Burt's been on a very rough book tour," Jay said, apologetically.

"I know!" I turned to Burt. "I once saw you on a PBS special. You were a nice guy then!"

"It's easy to be nice to nice people," he snarled.

"It is," I growled back.

"It's nice to see you two hit it off so well," Jay said.

Burt had his towel wrapped around his neck, his lips curled into a snarl.

"He's doing his Milton Berle impression, take a look at that," I said.

Jay cracked up, but the room was quiet. Whoops, I'd missed.

"Too obscure for the room," I said nervously, "anyway . . ."

"I'll bet that plays great on Nickelodeon," sneered Burt.

"At least *I* have a full-time job," I shot back.

"That's true . . ." Burt stopped mid-sentence. The two of us stared in disbelief. Jay walked toward us with what I could smell were pies made from shaving cream (an old show-biz trick) in his hands!

"What's this?" I protested, as Jay handed a pie to me and a pie to Burt.

"Shall we go back to back?" Burt said.

Before I knew what was happening, Burt and I were standing back to back with pies in our hands.

The band started a drum roll. Jay counted: "One, two . . ." We both spun before he got to three and smashed each other with pies. Mayhem erupted. There was shaving cream everywhere— on the wood floor, on the carpet, on the chairs, on me and Burt, everywhere except on Jay.

Burt hugged me, and then tried to hug Jay.

"Get away from me!" Jay said, running off stage into the band pit. It made me angry that Jay was clean. Johnny would have taken a pie; Johnny wasn't afraid to "pay off the joke." Jay was still too new to realize that getting dirty was part of the job. I was handed another pie. I said to the audience, "If I look like this and Burt looks like this . . ."

"Jay! Jay! Jay!" they chanted. They knew he should take one, too.

Jay appeared back onstage and managed to say into the camera, "Oh, ladies and gentlemen, we are out of time. We'll be right back *right* after these messages." He dashed away as Burt pitched shaving cream at his back.

We came back on the air for the show's wrapup. Staffers wiped me and Burt clean. Burt hugged me and whispered, "I only did that because I really like you."

What a liar, I thought.

Jay suggested Burt sign a copy of his book for me.

"What's your broad's name?" Burt asked me.

"What?"

"Your broad. Your wife."

Broad. Now that was a term I hadn't heard in several decades.

"To Marc and Alice," he wrote. "All my love, Burt." I kept the book, as a memento of the night. I've never read it.

Burt walked offstage, got into his limo, and left. He was out even before the cameras had stopped rolling. That's unheard of: everybody hangs out onstage and chats with Jay until taping's done.

Jay and I were out there alone. He leaned over, "What was that about?"

"I don't know."

"I don't know either," he said. "But I do know that whatever else it was, it was sure great television."

The cameras stopped rolling and I staggered offstage. What had just happened? I felt as though I'd just gone 10 rounds with Muhammad Ali, but I had no idea how I'd come off.

"That's either the best thing that's happened for my career or the worst" were the first words I said to my agent.

Jay's staff was nice enough to say that the show would replace my suit (I never took them up on it) and kept telling me that I'd be "on the anniversary reel."

Jay came into the dressing room to make sure I was okay. So did a couple of NBC executives. I suspected they were attorneys who were afraid I was going to sue. They left when they were satisfied that I hadn't been injured.

The taping finished at 6:30 P.M., but the show didn't broadcast until 11:30 that night. By the time I arrived home at 8:00, NBC was already running promos with me and Burt getting ready to kill each other with pies. I was so overwhelmed by the whole experience, I didn't even get into the shower. They had started running the promos on the East Coast, where the show airs three hours earlier, as soon as we stepped off the stage. This was hot stuff, and they knew it.

I sat with my family later that night and watched the show. Alice was speechless. Finally, my son Matthew said, "Dad, you should have let him hit you. Then you could have sued him and you'd never have to work again."

It wasn't until the next morning that everybody realized the magnitude of the stir the show had caused. Phone calls poured in. People assumed the routine had been set up: "stunting," as it's known in the industry.

"I'm not that good an actor," I protested. "If I were a trained performer, maybe I could have pulled it off. But I'm not! It was real!"

Within a week, the incident had been covered by every tabloid and all the news-magazine shows like *Hard Copy* and *Inside Edition.* "Burt Goes Berserk on *The Tonight Show!*" screamed a headline in the *New York Post.* I heard from my friend producer-director Steve Binder that Burt felt like he deserved more respect as a major movie star and that he had referred to me as a "bottom-feeder in show business." My mother called. "My God," she said. "What's this going to do for your career?"

"Good things!" I assured her.

Four years later I still get stopped in the street and asked about *The Tonight Show* with Burt Reynolds.

I'm sure Burt thought he deserved more respect, but the audience was cheering for me that night, not him.

And how was Jay through all this? After he mopped himself off, he didn't mind at all. It was the first time he had tied David

Letterman in the Nielsen ratings. And my Joseph Abboud suit? I had it dry-cleaned three times, until the smell of the shaving cream was finally gone. I haven't worn it since. It's still hanging, immaculate, in my closet. I keep it in there as a memorial to the event, a reminder of the bittersweet culmination of my childhood dream. I have no desire to wear it again, and no heart to throw it out.

M y admission that I was a "neatness fanatic" set off the fight with Burt, but it was barely noticed by the audience and completely ignored in the media coverage of our brawl. I later realized Burt had touched a nerve when he seized on that point and started needling me with it.

I didn't have a name for it at the time. I didn't know there was something called obsessive compulsive disorder. I didn't know that my fanatical neatness and propensity for lining things up at right angles were classic symptoms of OCD, a disorder I share with six million other Americans.

I was to learn that being a "neatness fanatic" was, in fact, only one of the many obsessions and compulsions that characterize my specific form of the disorder. I knew I was obsessed with neatness, but I had no idea that my obsession was clinical. I thought my obsessions were the normal type of day-to-day hang-ups the vast portion of humanity shares. But I was wrong. "Obsessions" for people with OCD are repetitive, intrusive, distressing, and anxiety-inducing thoughts. And "compulsions" are repetitive, ritualistic behaviors that we feel driven to perform in order to decrease our anxiety-provoking obsessive thoughts. The anxiety caused by obsessive thoughts is so strong that we repeatedly perform compulsive behaviors despite the fact that we don't enjoy performing them, and even though we're aware that our behavior makes no sense.

My obsessive need for order, symmetry, and exactness triggers my compulsion to align objects until everything is in its place. This is what I had been doing in *The Tonight Show* dressing room, arranging my bag on the couch and my magic props on the vanity table.

Obsessive compulsive disorder can be truly crippling, truly debilitating. People with OCD can become obsessed with contamination: the fear of dirt, germs, cancer, AIDS, bodily wastes, asbestos, poison, chemicals, radiation, and sticky substances or residues. Howard Hughes, a millionaire who once wined and dined with movie stars, was in later life so overwhelmed by his OCD- induced terror of germs that he sealed himself in one room. Servants, their hands covered with tissues, brought him his food. Hughes had curtains on all the windows to prevent sunlight from entering because he was afraid the sun might carry germs. He stored everything he was afraid might be "contaminated." He even saved his urine and feces in glass jars. My contamination obsessions are relatively benign. You'll read about my involved method of taking showers in hotel rooms so that my bare feet don't touch the floor. But that, fortunately, was about the extent of my contamination fears.

OCD sufferers can also be "hoarders": people who have trouble throwing things away because they feel they may need them later. Hoarders may save years of newspapers, and have no retrieval or filing system, but be unable to throw them out because they fear that someday they may need them. Some hoarders inspect household trash to make sure nothing "valuable" is being thrown out. I am fanatical about saving some things (I saved every paper from school since fourth grade, and have them stored in boxes), but I'm not the classic type of OCD hoarder, whose house or apartment is overflowing with junk.

Some people with OCD are besieged by thoughts of harming others. They fear that they will put poison in food, spread illness, smother a child, stab their spouse, push a stranger in front of a car, or run over a pedestrian. These people can become afraid to get into their cars for fear of hurting someone. I've never experienced these obsessive compulsive fears; but I have been convinced, as you'll see, that if I didn't practice certain rituals bad things would happen to me or to others (my plane would crash or my daughter wouldn't get a part in the school play, for example).

Another symptom I've experienced that is also common among OCD sufferers is an irrational urge to check things. For a brief period I was consumed by the thought that my car door was unlocked. I'd check it over and over. Others repeatedly check to make sure the stove isn't on or that they've turned off all the light switches before they leave the house. Anyone who's seen Jack Nicholson's Academy Award–winning portrayal of an obsessive compulsive sufferer in *As Good As It Gets* will remember his classic OCD checking antics: flipping the light switch on and off a certain number of times and locking and unlocking his door repeatedly.

Obsessions and compulsions that I've been lucky enough never to have experienced include: a fixation on lucky or unlucky numbers; religious obsessions and excessive moral concerns that lead to distressing "blasphemous" thoughts; repeatedly asking for reassurance; incessantly scrubbing one's hands; and, in more extreme cases, washing one's mouth out with Lysol because of contamination fears; counting things (signs along the highway or cracks in the sidewalk) or touching, rubbing, or tapping things (door frames, wall moldings). Radio and television personality Howard Stern admits that his OCD was once so severe that he was compelled to bang his head against the studio wall a certain number of times before each of his radio shows.

While almost everyone obsesses about something at one point or another in his or her life, people with OCD usually have multiple obsessions and compulsions. People are only considered to have OCD if their obsessions and compulsions are severe enough to cause them distress, consume an inordinate amount of their time, and interfere with their functioning in daily life. Like most OCD sufferers, I have found that performing compulsions does, briefly, alleviate anxiety; but the relief is temporary, and the anxiety-provoking obsessions quickly return, unabated.

In future chapters, we'll get into some of the science that concerns how and why the brains of people with OCD are different, and what happens in our brains when our symptoms occur. We'll see how tremendous advances in our understanding of OCD have helped to develop drug and behavior therapies that are extremely effective in treating our disorder.

On *The Tonight Show* with Burt Reynolds I had no idea that a chemical imbalance in my brain was what was causing me to be a neatness fanatic. But I did know that Burt had somehow cracked my public face, and underneath this carefully constructed public face lurked a very private torment. I had been tormented since I was a child with the constant anxiety of living in an inherently chaotic, imperfect world where I needed everything in its place. Most of the time that anxiety was at a low pitch. At other times it shrieked inside me like a siren. It was always there, lurking in the background.

I knew, intuitively, that this part of myself that needed everything in its place had a positive side. The same perfectionism that drove me to arrange my closet and dresser drawers like a drill sergeant's also spurred me on to succeed, to refuse to accept failure, to create for myself a public persona as a television performer in the brutally competitive world of show business. This public face was successful and self-assured. But this biggest night of my life in show business had opened a secret inner world that I had carried around inside me for nearly my whole life, since I was a very young child.

sunday, day of rest

Step on crack, break your Momma's back.
—*Anonymous children's rhyme*

On March 3, 1997, I appeared on *The Oprah Winfrey Show* with four other obsessive compulsive sufferers. Oprah, in a sleek black dress, made a dramatic entrance. The crowd, mostly female, leapt to its feet, hooting and whistling adoringly.

The crowd quieted, and Oprah read a page from the diary of Doron, one of my fellow guests on the show: "Today I went to the grocery store, and I was choosing a watermelon," Doron had written. "I felt gripped by fear. Someone had put poison in these watermelons and my fingerprints were all over them. I knew the police would accuse me of poisoning people who died after they ate these watermelons."

Knowing how difficult it was on a day-to-day basis for me to cope with the disorder, I wondered sadly how it was possible for someone as paranoid as Doron to function in the world. Doron was a perfectly normal-looking guy in his thirties, well-groomed with dark hair, wearing a black sweatshirt. I wondered how he felt about having his personal diary read aloud to 30 million Americans.

The first guest to appear on the show was Lorrie, who was so desperately afraid of contamination that she bathed in Lysol. Lorrie is a pretty woman in her mid-thirties with a sensitive face. Oprah showed a photo of her taken seven months earlier on her wedding day. She was radiant. But during those seven months the disorder had exploded, and the woman now facing Oprah was haggard and exhausted. She sat next to her husband Matt, weeping as Oprah ran film footage of what Lorrie went through each time she ate. Lorrie made Matt drive at least five miles from their house to buy her food. He had to inspect each item to make sure it was properly sealed. While Matt prepared her food, Lorrie locked herself in the bathroom, scrubbing her hands raw, "decontaminating" herself. Matt would lead her to the table, where she sat shaking and crying. Eyes scrunched shut, she forced each bite into her mouth. Eating was pure torture for her.

"I depend on my husband and my mom," Lorrie told Oprah. "I have no life. My rituals are my life. I spend all day decontaminating everything."

I hugged her, put my hand on her arm. Her white gloves were pulled up past the sleeves of her red dress that helped, along with a "force field" she imagined around her body, to protect her from germs. Oprah asked Lorrie if my hand was bothering her. She said no, but that if her skin had been exposed it would have.

"I recently came to a realization," Lorrie said. "My thoughts are what is contaminating me, not the things I think are contaminating me. I have to learn to live my life all over again."

Next on was Don, a "hoarder" who hadn't thrown anything away in 40 years. A clip ran of Don's apartment, so cluttered with his art collection, hats, bags and boxes of clothes, Christmas trees he'd never put together, every receipt he'd ever gotten, a Yogi Bear punching bag he'd had since he was 10 . . . endless stuff. Don, a balding man with glasses, told Oprah that he could manage the disorder on his own. But I suspected, as did everyone else watching, that his compulsion to hoard was out of control.

We broke for a commercial and I realized that this show wasn't like any other television program I'd ever appeared on or hosted. There was an ease and naturalness about it. I leaned toward Oprah. "I understand why you're such a hit. We're just *talking*."

"That's right, honey," she smiled. "We're just talking."

It was Oprah's birthday that day, and Julio Iglesias was going to come out and sing to her. But she opted to go with one more guest with OCD.

Much as I felt for Doron, Lorrie, and Don, it was Oprah's next guest who broke my heart. Eleven-year-old Darcie had her dark hair bound in a ponytail on top of her head. She reminded me of my daughter Meredith. But Meredith didn't wander through the house, checking all the electrical outlets and light switches, terrified of fire. Meredith wasn't desperately frightened of germs.

Meredith didn't constantly check herself in the mirror, some-times for hours on end, so worried about her appearance that she was often late for school.

"I get stuck in the mirror and have a hard time getting out," Darcie said, fighting back tears. "I know I look okay but I don't feel right. I don't feel comfortable if I leave. To people who hear this it might sound strange. When you have OCD you know how it feels."

I hugged Darcie before we went to commercial break. Oprah told her how brave she was to be there. "You're my hero for the day," she said.

She was my hero, too. My anxieties and compulsions as a child were not as crippling as Darcie's. But I knew what it was like to be consumed by doubts and fears. My childhood hadn't been particularly traumatic. But my OCD made it peculiar, per-haps even bizarre.

I grew up in a one-story limestone house in the northern part of the city of Indianapolis. My family had a one-acre lot, so our side yard was big enough for a good game of baseball or football. There were always a million kids around. One neighbor, David Rust, had a basketball court, so every day after dinner we'd go over to his house and play. Or, if David didn't want to play, there was another court behind the field in back of our house, near the farmers' pump house.

Every Sunday, after Sunday school, my brother, sister, and I came home and changed into our play clothes. Except I didn't play. Instead, I'd kick my older brother Mike out of the room we shared and start to clean. As my brother eagerly ran to watch TV or outside to play football, I'd turn on the radio or my little portable TV and shut the bedroom door. From the time I was eight years old until I was sixteen, every single Sunday of my life I cleaned everything in exactly the same way in exactly the same order.

This was no ordinary cleaning. First I'd strip my bunk bed, and dust the woodwork behind the bed and the bed itself. I'd walk around and around the bed as I made it, back and forth, until the bedding was perfectly smooth and symmetrical. The bedspread couldn't touch the floor. It had to be perfectly even along the bottom. I put the bed back into its indentations in our dark green carpet so I wouldn't make new ones. If, by chance, the bed had left any slight indentations in its temporary position, I would get down on my hands and knees and rub them out.

I then turned my attention to our bookshelf. I dusted each book with a rag—the cover, binding, spine, bottom, top, every surface. I dusted and Pledged the shelves, put each book back in its place, taking care that the edges were exactly flush with the lip of the bookshelf. The bookshelf alone could take an hour to clean.

On top of my brother's dresser was the stereo our dad had given him; he hated for me to touch it. "Keep your hands off my stuff," he'd say. But when it came to cleanliness, the room was my territory. I *needed* to dust underneath that stereo. I *had to* angle its hinged speakers in a particular direction.

To the right of the dresser was a bulletin board. It wasn't like other kids' bulletin boards with everything overlapping and helter skelter. My bulletin board was perfectly symmetrical, with all the items radiating in equidistant perfection from the big photo of Johnny Carson at the center. Below the bulletin board was the desk I shared with my brother. I would dust the desk drawers and then turn my attention to the dresser.

At age 11, I came to the earth-shattering realization that "balling" my socks would stretch out their elastic, so I began folding them. This made it possible to stack them. Browns with browns, blues with blues, blacks with blacks. My ties, belts, play pants, and T-shirts were all organized and folded according to a system that I still use today. My good clothes were hung exactly an inch and a half apart in my closet, organized by function and color. They all faced (and face) the same direction. I hung my pants perfectly, always folding them carefully to avoid the dreaded double-crease.

Once a month, I'd binge, moving everything away from the walls and dusting behind the furniture. My mother called those Sundays "spring cleaning." Sometimes, a rag would come up with so much dust that I'd run to show it off to Mom. "Oh, look at that!" she'd exclaim. My mother never once had to say, "You'd better go to your room and clean." She realized how important cleaning was to me and accepted me as a quirky, clean little boy. There was nothing in my room that wasn't Pledged to death, wiped, Windexed, vacuumed. Nothing. Everything was shiny and perfect. I loved the way a clean room smelled. Cleaning gave me an incredible feeling of satisfaction. It fulfilled a very deep inner need.

Occasionally, my mother or father would stick their head in to see how I was doing. I barely glanced up. I was completely focused. Even at that young age, I needed absolute order. I needed to do things in a way that felt right. I needed to have everything in its place.

Cleaning was a recreational activity for me and my mother. I'd help her buff our floors until they shined, and she loved the way I vacuumed the house. As a kid I didn't think, "Let me do this so I can get rid of this horrible knot in my stomach," which is what I thought later in life. I enjoyed my cleaning rituals more as a child than later as an adult, when I derived no pleasure from carrying out my compulsions; when they became just a source of pain. I fondly remember cleaning with my mother as a child. Mom and I had a special bond that I don't think she shared with my brother Mike or my sister Lori.

A couple times a year I'd clean all the windows in the house, inside and out. I'd be up on a ladder and Mom would stand inside and point out dirt as I cleaned. My mother's special attention was particularly important to me because I was intensely competitive with my older brother Mike. His IQ was off the charts, and he had a photographic memory.

It wasn't Mike's intelligence I envied, however. He had played the drums from a very early age, and was a child prodigy. At 15, he was on the road with Henry Mancini and Johnny Mathis, and playing The Embers, the biggest nightclub in Indianapolis, when he was still underage. I envied him because he was closer to show business than I was. He hung out with celebrities. I eagerly drank up his stories of the people he'd met. While I dreamt show business, he lived it.

My father worked seven days a week at Berkys Supermarket, which my grandfather built and owned. The store closed at 8 P.M.

and Dad would usually be home by 9:00. If he wasn't, my mother would begin to pace and wring her hands.

"Oh my god! Where is your father?" she'd moan.

By 9:20, she'd panic. Passing headlights sent her running to the dining room window.

"Is that your father? Is it? Oh, no. Maybe he's had an accident! Let's call the hospital. Let's call the police."

My brother would roll his eyes and shoot her a "get a life" look. My sister was oblivious. But my mother's hysterics turned me into a wreck. I agonized about my father. Was he okay? Had something happened? As my mother paced, I paced right behind her. I prayed Dad wasn't dead.

Then, inevitably, headlights would swoop into our driveway, the garage door would swing open, and in would walk Dad.

"Where were you?" Mom would ask.

"Lois," he'd say, "I was working. Traffic was heavy."

"I thought something happened to you! I was so worried."

He'd sigh. "It's been a long day. Where's my dinner?"

Without further ado, he'd sit down at the table and eat the dinner she had prepared.

In some ways, I think my mom's behavior may have triggered my OCD. Although she's never been officially diagnosed, I believe she was (and is) afflicted by the disorder. She was a constant worrier, and, like many OCD sufferers, when she was under stress her symptoms flared. When Mom slipped into her obsessive compulsive behavior it seemed to bring out the same feelings in me.

Although I had specific types of anxieties, they didn't generalize to make me a fearful person. My mother picked up on my outgoing, uninhibited personality early on and encouraged it. She gave me my start in show business. Even as a toddler I loved to perform. I was always animated—like a cartoon character. I had no fear.

I was infatuated with television. One day when I was four or five my mother whisked me off to the NBC affiliate in Indianapolis to audition for *Romper Room,* one of the first educational shows on TV. I hit it off with the show's host, Miss Sue, and immediately appeared for a week on the program. I did so well that I became a fill-in for absent kids.

The coolest thing on the show was the magic mirror. Miss Sue would look into the mirror and say, "Romper Stomper Bomper Boo!" As she said it, film rolled in weird, psychedelic patterns. Then she held the mirror, now only a frame. You could see clear through to the other side. In the studio, I watched the stage manager run over and switch Miss Sue's mirrors. The studio had a particular smell, a sweet smell with a hint of electricity behind it. There was a tremendous soothing heat from the intense lights. To me, the studio smelled like burning Graham Crackers.

I subbed on *Romper Room* for a couple of years and became completely hooked on entertaining and performing, on the power and prestige of being on television. Even at the time, television was the only place I felt totally comfortable. At school, on the playground, at home, I always felt slightly on edge, as though I was on the verge of disaster: a drink spilled on my pants, my father coming late, dust behind my bureau.

My doctor and I think my feeling of comfort on TV is linked to my OCD. When I'm on television I'm in charge, in control. On camera, I never perform obsessive compulsive rituals. I can be a "normal" person. Television is like dream time or fantasy time for me, a hyper-reality. When the cameras start to roll I walk out of this world onto another planet. I am like the stutterer who stops stuttering when he starts to sing. Internally, I know I'm still fighting the demon of the disorder. But I don't have to fight it when I'm on television. I have felt that way since my Romper Room days. Performance has always been therapeutic for me. I'm completely in the moment, in the zone, all my attention focused on how I'm doing.

This kind of shifting of attention away from obsessive compulsive rituals and thought patterns is the thrust of behavior therapy, a powerful OCD treatment I'll discuss later in this book. When you shift focus, and become totally concentrated on something outside normal day-to-day activities, it's impossible to be run by obsessions and compulsions.

The first time I realized the full force of the freedom I felt from the disorder was when I was onstage. I was six years old. My parents took me to an ice show in Chicago. After the show, the M.C. encouraged kids to come up and tell jokes onstage.

"Tell a joke," he said, "and you can put your hand in our penny jar and keep whatever you can grab."

Without asking my parents, I slid from my seat. In a split second, I was standing next to a tall man in a tuxedo. Without a trace of nervousness, I told my joke: "If two planes crash in mid-air, where do they bury the survivors?"

"I don't know," the M.C. said. "Where?"

"They don't bury the survivors, only the dead people!"

I heard a tremendous roar of laughter.

At that moment I knew that this was what I wanted to do with the rest of my life. I wanted to be onstage, telling jokes or performing.

I stuck my hand in the big fishbowl filled to the brim with pennies. For good measure, I stuck my other hand in, too. With my two little fists filled with pennies, I ran back to my seat. My parents were rolling with laughter.

That was my first paid gig. I relived it in my mind, over and over. I experienced the same rush each time I pictured it. I dreamt about getting back onstage and getting that feeling again.

The Delaware Trail Elementary School was a block and a half from our house. My trip was five minutes shorter if I cut through the grass, but if I did that I'd get dew on my shiny leather shoes and my nicely creased pants. If my shoes got wet on the way to school, I went straight to the bathroom, pulled paper towels from the dispenser, and wiped them until they were bone-dry. After recess on the gravel playground, I ran into the bathroom and cleaned the dirt and dust off my shoes until I could see my face in them. If I got ink on my hands, I washed it off immediately. Lots of kids wrote on their hands—a repugnant thought! Dirt under my nails? Horrors! But not as terrible as ink on my clothes. I'd keep staring and staring at the stain. It was all I thought about for the rest of the day. I couldn't wait to get home and give the clothes to Mom to wash.

Despite these childhood "quirks," I was a popular kid. In Indianapolis in the early '60s, being a jock was the key to being well-liked. I loved sports, and I was good at them. I played in Little League and made the All-Star team several years in a row. I enjoyed and excelled at track and field. I never had trouble making friends.

I was in the Cub Scouts, and once a month my pack had inspection. We stood at attention and the pack leader would walk the line, scrutinizing us. Were our neckerchiefs properly rolled? Did our shoes shine? At home, there was a shoe-shine kit in the laundry room. Black wax, a polish brush, a buffer. I'd brush my uniform shoes until they glowed. Then I'd have shoe polish under my nails. I'd scrub them for 15 minutes until the polish was completely gone.

The scout who won inspection always got a gold medal. Well, it was more like a key chain. But to me, it was a gold medal. I had a ton of them. My whole two years in Cub Scouts I never lost an inspection. Not once. I'm very competitive: To this day my kids hate to play Monopoly or Scrabble with me. I'm a *pain.* I tell them I'm going to crush them. I rag them to death. I do whatever it takes to win.

Whether playing Monopoly or climbing the show business ladder, I have to be the best. This obsession with winning is part of the constellation of symptoms of OCD. It's part of my drive to be perfect. The drive to win, to be perfect, to be the best can be a positive. It can motivate people to pay attention, to struggle and not give up in pursuit of their goals. This is why I think that most CEOs in corner offices probably have a touch of OCD.

But there is a downside to this perfectionism. It can be crippling. Many people with OCD become so stressed-out and overwhelmed with their need to be perfect that they don't take on new things. An obsessive compulsive sufferer who gets straight-A grades in college may decide not to go to graduate school because he's afraid of not performing up to his undergraduate standard. This kind of thinking can prevent some perfectionist OCD sufferers from taking on new challenges.

Perfectionism can be a terrible burden, but it spurs me on. I'm driven to achieve, and I'm also a risk-seeker. I'm not terrified of losing; just intent on winning. Although I'm driven to be perfect, I survive when I suffer setbacks or fail. My life hasn't been a smooth upward progression, but I've shrugged it off when things haven't worked out for me. To my fellow obsessive compulsive sufferers I say: You too can learn to deal with adversity. You may have an extraordinary need to be perfect, but take that as a challenge, not a burden. Fight hard, and if you don't succeed, don't get caught up in a sense of failure. Go on to the next challenge, and put everything you have into meeting it. Then move on.

Typical of perfectionist OCD sufferers, even as a child I made lists all the time. There was always a pad of paper or an index card near my glasses on the night table. I'd often get out of bed after I'd turned off the light to write things on my list. When I woke up, I looked at my list: "Study for history test. Baseball practice 3 to 4. Call Mr. Kubit about props at 5."

If I didn't write it down, I was sure I'd forget it. Never mind that I kept a running list in my head that I recited like a litany, over and over again during the day. I doubt there was any chance that I would forget anything, list or no. I checked things off as I accomplished them. Looking back, that was pure OCD.

What I take to be my "manageable" obsessive compulsive

childhood traits—neatness, list-making, punctuality, infatuation with performing—had a darker side. On *Oprah* that day in 1997, as I listened to Darcie talk about her fears, I was taken back to feelings in my own childhood. Like Darcie, I was consumed by anxieties that were deeply disturbing. They began when I empathized with my mother's fear that when my father was late, it meant he'd been in an accident.

But my anxieties began to escalate. I thought my parents would die if I didn't do everything in exactly the right way. When I took my glasses off at night I'd have to place them on the dresser at a particular angle. Sometimes I'd turn on the light and get out of bed seven times until I felt comfortable with the angle. If the angle wasn't right, I felt that my parents would die. The feeling ate up my insides.

If I didn't grab the molding on the wall just the right way as I entered or exited my room; if I didn't hang a shirt in the closet perfectly; if I didn't read a paragraph a certain way; if my hands and nails weren't perfectly clean, I thought my incorrect behavior would kill my parents.

I didn't know why I was thinking these awful things. Where did these thoughts come from? Why was I saying all this to myself? "They're going to die. They're going to die," kept running through my head. "I've killed them. It's my fault!"

I started to wonder if other people had these feelings and intrusive thoughts. I knew that if I asked others, though, and it turned out they didn't share my feelings, they'd think I was crazy. So I kept these thoughts secret. Years later I learned that children with OCD commonly involve their families in their rituals (they demand, for example, that dishes be washed repeatedly).

But not me. Not only did I not want anyone else to physically take part in my rituals, I didn't want even my closest family members to know about them.

I was scared to death. I thought I was nuts. I knew the stuff I was doing was weird, and I was afraid that if I mentioned my strange thoughts to my parents they'd send me to a psychiatrist. And back then, in 1964, if you went to a psychiatrist, you were insane. Looking back, even if I had asked my parents for help, there was not a chance my mother would ever have sent me to that kind of doctor. And, come to think of it, if I had said to my parents, "I have these feelings that if I don't clean up perfectly something bad will happen," they would have said, "Yeah, so? What's the problem?" I believe now that both my parents had the disorder, so there was no way they would have seen my obsessive compulsive behavior as evidence that I needed help.

The rare occasions when I failed to perform a ritual or complete a task were sheer nightmares. I would wake up in the middle of the night and lie there, consumed by fear. I'd sneak out of bed, careful not to wake my brother, and tiptoe down the hall. I'd stand in the doorway of my parents' room, listening for their breathing. It was cold and dark in the house. It was the dead hours of the night. No cars passed on the street. I could hear the faint humming of the refrigerator. I was terrified. I was convinced I had killed my parents because I hadn't cleaned my room thoroughly.

I wouldn't leave their doorway until I heard them both breathing. Often I would fall asleep standing up, leaning against the door frame, and my father would catch me and say, "What are you up to? Go to bed!" He always thought I was sleepwalking, but I was making sure that Mom and Dad were both still alive. When

I saw that they were, and that my "failure" didn't have terrible consequences, for a brief time—perhaps a week or two, sometimes longer—the fears would decrease.

After we finished the *Oprah* show I offered to go visit Darcie Kahn at her elementary school in Lawrence, Massachusetts. She told me the kids in her fifth-grade class had been bothering her. She had seen a doctor who recommended that she try to alleviate her classmates' teasing by talking to them about OCD. But that had only made matters worse. Boys had been tormenting her, making cruel remarks about her OCD. She thought my presence in her classroom might help dispel some of the cruelty directed toward her, and I was glad to help.

The thought of Darcie having to cope with the ridicule of classmates on top of everything else she was going through made me shudder. As a kid I'd managed to hide my behaviors from my parents, siblings, teachers, and schoolmates. Darcie's openness impressed me.

I flew to Boston and then drove to Lawrence. I met first with the principal of the school, who asked if the kids would know who I was.

"I think so," I said.

Word had gotten out among the students that I was in the building. As I accompanied the principal to Darcie's classroom the halls were buzzing, kids sticking their heads out of doors, whispering and pointing. The school began to go wild. (Apparently they knew who I was!)

In Darcie's classroom we talked about how everyone was different, and how we need to appreciate each other's differences because that's what makes humanity rich. Darcie said later that my visit made a big difference in the way she was treated by her peers. Meeting a successful television personality with OCD helped the kids realize that suffering from the disorder doesn't mean you're weird or bad.

Darcie's family, however, continues to struggle. Her younger sister Teal has just been diagnosed with OCD. Beatrice, her mother, said that on a recent family vacation to Florida, Teal came down with strep throat. She ran a high fever, wasn't eating, and, within a few days, had full-blown OCD. (Later on, we'll discuss how strep triggers the disorder.)

Suddenly, Teal refused to wear her shoes and socks. She couldn't stand to have her clothing touch her waist. At night, she now has an overwhelming fear of fire. She won't go to sleep. Either Beatrice or her husband Marty has to stay up with Teal until she's utterly exhausted and passes out in their arms. During the day, Teal walks around the house with a Windex bottle in her hand, cleaning everything in sight.

"It's hard," says Beatrice. "But we'll get through it."

Beatrice and Marty are fantastic examples of how parents of children with OCD can respond to the disorder. "I'm not ashamed of my children," says Beatrice. "I would fight for them tooth and nail. I want them to feel proud of themselves. They're great kids!"

The Kahns are trying to find the right medication at the right dosage for Teal. When they do, they're confident her symptoms will decrease. Darcie says that while medication has helped her, it hasn't cured her. She's in behavior therapy, which she says can be pure torture, but which has been beneficial. In the past, she picked her arms until they were covered with scabs. This "picking" is actually a symptom of another disorder that is closely related to and often accompanies OCD. The behavior therapy got Darcie to wait to pick—first 10, then 20, then 30 minutes—until the urge diminished.

Darcie has told me that her therapy has made her confront her fears. "It's been hard work," she says, "and nerve-wracking. But each time I do it I become a little stronger."

Darcie and her family have been an inspiration to me and, I'm sure, to many others. Even if I had known in fifth grade that I had OCD, I would never have had the courage to stand before my class, describe my symptoms, and ask for help in my struggle to overcome them.

Can you imagine anything braver than that?

| *three* |

nurture and nature

DOCTOR: Look, how she rubs her hands.

GENTLEWOMAN: It is an accustomed action . . . I have known her to continue in this a quarter of an hour.

LADY MACBETH: Yet here's a spot. . . . Out, damned spot! out, I say! . . .What, will these hands never be clean?

— Shakespeare, *Macbeth* (Act 5, Scene I)

Dr. Hollander tells me scientists believe that OCD can run in families, passed down from generation to generation. My family history certainly bears out this theory.

My mother's parents came from Russia and Romania to Toledo, Ohio, where they owned a laundry. I was five when my mother's father died. Every summer after my grandmother was widowed, I took a six-hour bus ride to Toledo to stay with her for two or three weeks. My cousins lived down the block, and we would ride our bikes to the zoo together, beneath the shade trees, down the wide sidewalks. Grandma would send me to the grocery store, and she always let me keep the change.

My grandmother liked her windows spotless. As she got older, she had trouble stepping up on the ladder, so she would wait for me to come visit, and we'd clean them together. It was exactly the same routine that I did with my Mom. My grandmother would stand inside, pointing out dirt, as I cleaned outside. I loved it.

Grandma had a chrome breakfast-room table and chairs, and she had somehow figured out that rubbing the chrome with wax paper made it shine. She'd give me sheets of wax paper, and I'd get down on my hands and knees and rub the chairs and the base of that table until they sparkled in the sunlight.

As soon as you walked in the front door of her house you were overpowered by the smell of mothballs coming from a closet where winter coats were stored. People with OCD believe in overkill: if five mothballs are enough, fifteen are even better. So it was with Grandma.

On hot summer nights, my grandmother and I would sit out on the front porch. Grandma would sweep the sidewalk and street with her old-fashioned straw broom before coming onto the porch and settling into her glider. She'd start from the bottom of the porch stairs and, with short vigorous strokes, sweep every inch of pavement in front of the house. When she was done, not one leaf or speck of dirt remained. Relatives would stop by and chat. We would wait for the street lights to come on, and then go inside to watch TV, or walk to the drug store to get ice cream.

My other grandparents were also neatness fanatics. Their house in Indianapolis was perfect. They kept slippery plastic seat covers on their '56 Pontiac: heaven forbid the upholstery should get dirty. We never sat in their living room. The only time I remember being in that room was when my grandmother died. I distinctly recall a bowl of living-room candy, red peppermints with white stripes, that nobody ever touched. Both my grandparents' homes had a museum feel. Looking back on what I know about them and what my parents have told me, I feel quite certain that both my grandmothers and my father's father had OCD.

My parents, too, may be afflicted with the disorder. You've already heard about my mother's cleaning compulsions and OCD anxieties, and my father is also not a stranger to OCD symptoms. His closet is perfect, impeccable, like a fancy men's clothing store. It's amazing, a work of art. Every suit, every tie, every shirt is in perfect order. It looks like my own closet! When I was child, we had a cleaning woman come once a week. "Tell Laura not to touch my closet," my dad would say. If she moved a pair of his shoes a millimeter, he knew. Everything had its place and belonged in a certain order.

Our entire house was pretty much like that. I used to joke in my comedy routines that when I got up at night and went to the bathroom, I'd come back to find my bed had been made. I'd also joke that my mother put paper under the cuckoo clock. OCD has rich material for a comic! Growing up in a house like that didn't really bother me or my brother or sister—I just felt that other people's homes were a little different.

It has taken my parents several years since I outed myself on *Biggers and Summers* to recognize the OC part of their personalities. Initially, they resented my "airing my dirty laundry" and, by extension, *their* dirty laundry in public. They said there was absolutely no way they were afflicted with the disorder. I think deep down they blamed themselves for my condition and felt a tremendous amount of guilt. But as I have continued to campaign with the OC Foundation, my parents have come around. My mother brags to anyone and everyone about how many people I've helped. And the last time I was in Indianapolis, both my parents admitted that they "might have a touch" of the disorder.

So it seems that I got OCD genes from both sides of my family—a double whammy. What does it mean that "I got OCD genes from both sides of the family?" How does genetic inheritance work? I'm not an expert in the genetics or neurochemistry of OCD, but I've had extensive conversations with Dr. Hollander, who is, and I've tried to boil down what I've learned from him into layman's language.

When a sperm fertilizes an egg and creates a fetus, the cells of that fetus have their own set of genes, half from Mom and half from Dad. In identical twins, the original cell splits in half, and each grows into a separate person with identical gene sets. When two separate sperm fertilize two different eggs, fraternal (nonidentical) twins result, who are no more genetically related than any two siblings.

In a disease that is 100 percent genetically inherited, if one identical twin has the disease, the other twin will have it, because they have the exact same set of genes. But this doesn't seem to be the case with OCD. According to Dr. Hollander, OCD does have a genetic component, but researchers agree it is less than 100 percent. No "OCD gene" has been identified, and researchers generally agree that it is likely that more than one gene is involved in developing the disorder.

Studies are currently under way that may untangle the genetic causes of OCD. These studies involve hundreds of families with more than one OCD sufferer. Blood is taken from all family members and analyzed in a "gene scanner" to determine the entire content of each person's gene set. Comparing this information to whether or not each individual has OCD will enable researchers to determine which genes play roles in the development of the disorder.

Because several genes probably act together to produce OCD, isolating OCD genes is tough. To further complicate matters, the different varieties of OCD may each be brought about by different sets of genes. Dr. Hollander speculates that my subgroup of OCD, characterized by need for order and symmetry, is inherited through different genes than the OCD of people with, for instance, contamination fears. Pinpointing all the involved genes will probably take at least five more years. But the results will be worth waiting for: the disorder may be able to be treated, perhaps even cured, with new medications or with gene therapy.

Some subgroups of OCD—like my everything has-to-be-in-its-place-type—seem to have a larger genetic component than other subgroups. My type of OCD generally begins in childhood, and it mostly occurs in boys. People with my type of OCD want things to be perfect; symmetry is crucial to us. Repetitive touching, counting, tapping, eye blinking, shrugging, humming, and throat clearing are also common to my OCD type, although I never experienced these symptoms. People with adult-onset OCD are more likely to be women concerned with harm avoidance. These people are more worried that something bad will happen to someone close to them, and they are more likely to develop compulsions to ward off future ills. I have no idea why this is so, and neither do the most informed researchers. No one yet understands the gender breakdown, although it is generally accepted that OCD affects males and females in equal numbers.

Researchers have learned that having the OCD gene or genes does not necessarily mean you'll develop the disorder; environmental factors also contribute to whether a person develops or does not develop OCD. It seems likely I was genetically prone to OCD, but what was it about my environment that encouraged me to develop the disorder? According to Dr. Hollander, some researchers think certain types of personalities are prone to OCD. Eagerness to please and a tendency to feel responsible for others—both traits I had as a child (and still have)—may have predisposed me to the disorder. Being shy also may make a person more likely to develop OCD. I haven't been shy a day in my life, which goes to show you that these are all possible tendencies, not hard-and-fast rules.

Parents who are worriers, who are always afraid something terrible may happen (my mom, for example), may contribute to their children getting OCD. Growing up in an exceptionally rigid household, which I did not, with parents who demand their children stick to routines and do things until they're done perfectly, may also encourage a child to develop OCD. A stressful event, such as the death of a loved one, can trigger the onset of the disorder. Children, especially, may be sensitive to death or separation; in some cases it seems to sensitize them to the idea that bad things can happen. Sometimes children are haunted by this knowledge and may try to develop some sort of "protection" against the fundamental uncertainties of life, which can lead to the performance of magical rituals to ward off harm, and full-blown OCD.

OCD is found in people worldwide, often at the same rate as in the United States: 2 to 3 percent of the population. The symptoms suffered by a peasant living in a remote village in India and a businessman in downtown Tokyo are often similar: the peasant may fear he's contaminating his food with dirty fingers; the businessman with dirty chopsticks. Religious and cultural beliefs influence OCD: devout Catholics may compulsively confess, Protestants may suffer blasphemous urges at prayer time, orthodox Jews may be consumed with keeping the strict laws of Kosher, Moslems may pray excessively to Mecca.

OCD has plagued people for centuries. As far back as the Middle Ages, church writings vividly described monks, priests, and laypeople suffering from blasphemous thoughts, demoralizing indecision, compulsive scripture reading, and pathological doubting. It is now believed that many of these people were suffering from OCD. At the time, it was believed that these people were possessed by the devil, who besieged them with blasphemous or aggressive images. People were sometimes burned at the stake for these supposed demonic possessions.

Perhaps when Shakespeare created the character of Lady Macbeth he was responding to the medieval idea that OCD and the devil are intimately entwined. This character, Shakespeare's immortal depiction of evil incarnate, may have suffered from OCD. Dr. Hollander believes she was a compulsive hand washer. She had no insight into her condition, and while this is unusual for people with the disorder, it is not unheard of: about 5 percent of OCD sufferers are delusional.

In 1909, Sigmund Freud wrote a famous OCD case history: "Notes Upon a Case of Obsessional Neurosis," as the disorder was then known. He described the case of "Rat Man," a young, well-educated patient who suffered from blasphemous and sexual obsessions and vivid, recurring images of rats devouring him and his father. Freud attributed these symptoms to failures in toilet training and a regression back to infantile Oedipal urges, an explanation that held for much of this century.

Fortunately, in the last 15 years, psychiatrists and neuroscientists have made tremendous advances in understanding OCD. 15 years! That's nothing. Imagine: if I'd gone to a psychiatrist in 1970, even in the unlikely event I was diagnosed with OCD, it would have done me no good. I would have been treated with traditional psychoanalysis. The theory then was that if the underlying psychological problem could be understood and treated, the obsessive compulsive symptoms would vanish. It's ironic that traditional psychoanalysis, far from improving my symptoms, might actually have made them worse. Delving into the "meaning" of my obsessive thoughts might have encouraged me to attribute significance to them, exacerbating the anxiety they provoked in me and causing me to increase my ritualistic behaviors. The doctor might have convinced me that I had obsessive fears of my plane crashing because I secretly wanted to die, instead of helping me understand that these intrusive thoughts were a meaningless reflection of the imbalance in my brain chemistry.

The Freudian explanation for OCD has now been thoroughly debunked by science. Although many questions remain, it's now been proven that OCD is caused by a biological imbalance in the brain.

As is true with many medical problems, doctors are better at treating OCD than they are at understanding what's happened to create the condition or how the drugs work that help people get better. The first clue to what's actually going on in the brains of OCD sufferers was discovered because researchers noticed that OCD symptoms responded well to a medication whose effects on a different ailment were already known. In 1986, an exploration was made into the effect of a drug called Anafranil on OCD sufferers. Seventy-percent of OCD patients responded to treatment with Anafranil, which affects the serotonin system in the brain. This was a tremendous discovery. For the first time, doctors realized OCD was a treatable illness. At the same time it was discovered that this disorder was twice as common as the better-known psychiatric disorders of schizophrenia, bipolar disorder, and panic disorder, each of which is present in only 1 percent of our population. Two to 3 percent of Americans have OCD.

Since manipulating the body's serotonin levels worked to alleviate OCD symptoms, scientists assumed the cause of OCD must have something to do with this chemical substance. Serotonin is found in the billions of nerve cells, or neurons, in our brains. A neuron consists of a cell body and lots of tentacles, the longest of which is the axon. The tiny gap between the end of one axon and the next neuron is a synapse. An impulse begins in a neuron's cell body and travels to the tip of its axon. The impulse is then transferred into chemical messengers, called neurotransmitters, which are released into the synapse. These neurotransmitters cross the synapse and stimulate, or tickle, receptors on the receiving neuron. After they've done their duty, the neurotransmitters are usually taken back up by the neuron that released them. If enough receptors are stimulated on a receiving neuron, it will fire, and the impulse will continue along its way.

All this happens very quickly—impulses travel along some neural pathways at speeds over 200 miles per hour. Along with telling neurons to fire, a critical job of our brain is telling them *not* to fire. Many neurotransmitters are "inhibitory": they carry a message that discourages the receiving neuron from firing. If there weren't inhibitors and even a small fraction of our neurons were allowed to fire simultaneously, we would be completely unable to function.

Serotonin is one of the many different neurotransmitters that help our nerve cells "talk" to each other. It plays a role in regulating anxiety, appetite, sex drive, and mood. It also plays a role in assessing danger in the environment, and, by affecting the rate at which neurons fire, it modulates the activity of different brain regions. In the brains of people with OCD, something seems to have gone awry with the serotonin system. Only no one's really sure what. It's not as simple as having too much or too little serotonin. It seems likely that the receptors serotonin stimulates after crossing synapses are overly sensitive, so the brain has an exaggerated response to serotonin, which may help account for the constant sense of danger OCD sufferers feel. A small percentage of OCD patients don't seem to have anything wrong with their serotonin systems, further complicating matters. It seems likely that other neurotransmitters, such as dopamine, are also involved in OCD.

Not only is the serotonin system awry in most OCD sufferers, but different parts of the brain seem to have gone into overdrive. In the 1990s, studies have been done with technologies that allow researchers to actually see inside the brain. CAT scans (computerized axial tomography) and MRIs (magnetic resonance imaging) provide X-ray-like pictures that reveal the brain's structure, while PET scans (positron emission tomography), EEGs, and computer-assisted EEGs (electroencephalograms) allow researchers to observe brain activity.

Using this technology, researchers have learned that in people with OCD, three regions of the brain seem to be hyperactive. The first is the orbital-frontal cortex, the outer layer of our brain just above our eyes. This region is involved in assessing danger in the environment and planning behavior to respond to it. The orbital-frontal cortex is part of the most highly evolved region of our brain, which separates us from all other creatures. The second hyperactive region is the head of the caudate nucleus, part of the basal ganglia, a small cluster of cells buried deep within the brain. The basal ganglia is involved in coordinating movement. This is what enables us to learn to do something automatically after repeated practice. And, finally, the thalamus and anterior cingulate, located directly above the spinal cord, are overactive in OCD sufferers. These structures are part of the limbic system, the deepest and most primitive part of our brain. They are involved in driving the primitive impulses of emotion, sex, aggression, and anxiety.

Not only do these three brain regions seem to be overactive in OCD patients, but they seem to act in concert—not the normal state of affairs. Normally, these different regions fulfill their separate tasks independently. Using PET scans, researchers were able to monitor brain activity when OCD patients were presented with stimuli designed to provoke their anxiety (a towel dipped in a toilet bowl, for example). All three regions flared up, the neurons firing like crazy. Serotonin seems to play an important role in the regulation of this pathway and in "locking" these brain regions together. After an OCD patient has been successfully treated and balance has been restored to his serotonin system, PET scans have demonstrated that these regions return to normal: they decrease in activity and are no longer locked together in action.

Every time people with OCD respond to an obsessive thought by performing a ritual, they strengthen the brain circuit connecting the frontal cortex, the basal ganglia, and the thalamus—in effect worsening their symptoms. An OCD patient develops a "habit memory," akin to what happens when you learn to ride a bike or learn a new dance step. When you first try a new dance step, you have to think about it, about where each foot goes and in what order. The longer you practice, the less you have to think. In a practiced dancer, the steps become automatic, become a habit memory, "etched" into the brain.

The basal ganglia is instrumental in developing these habit memories. This part of the brain seems to be at the root of the trouble in OCD—when damage is done to it directly, through disease or injury, people who previously had no trace of OCD sometimes develop the disorder. This is what can happen when a child gets strep throat. Occasionally, the antibodies produced to kill off the strep infection actually start to attack the child's body. Sometimes the antibodies attack the basal ganglia. It's just been discovered that this attack, which leaves the basal ganglia bulging and inflamed, can kick in the hyperactive loop between the three regions of the brain involved in OCD.

Remember Darcie, my 11-year-old hero from the *Oprah* show? That is likely what happened to her five-year-old sister, who developed severe OCD immediately after becoming ill with strep throat. In fact, strep throat may be the precipitating factor in some of kids who develop OCD. To Darcie's family, and to me, the most exciting aspect of this discovery is that these special cases of OCD may be treatable and even preventable with antibiotics.

I think it's occurred to some of us with OCD to ask why we all have such similar obsessions and compulsions. Many, many people with OCD feel a compulsion to check to see if the stove is on. Why not have a compulsion to continuously dance? Or to continually write? Or climb trees? Why not get obsessed with money? Or with love? Why are we so consumed with fear? Why don't we feel overwhelmed by the compulsion to tell everyone how much we love them? Why do so many of us wash our hands until they're raw? Why do we feel compelled to order only our own belongings, but not other people's? Why are we consumed with order and not chaos? And why are OCD symptoms so similar regardless of cultural environment?

The typical concerns of OCD, which at first seem like such a hodgepodge of symptoms, can actually be grouped together in a few categories—hygiene, territorial order, sex, and aggression. These concerns are the same basic impulses or instincts found in many lower species (birds, dogs, and lizards, for example) and they seem to be hard-wired into our limbic system.

All animals engage in primitive fixed action patterns, which include grooming, nest building, reproducing, and defending territory. These primitive fixed actions are instinctual. They help species survive. Sometimes, something goes wrong with these instinctual behaviors. Acral lick syndrome in dogs is an example of this: the dog cleans itself with its tongue until it has no fur left. Parrots sometimes get a disorder in which they pluck all their feathers out. Animals suffering these disorders engage in pathological grooming—they're performing their primitive fixed actions excessively, causing themselves harm. Researchers have found that the same medications that relieve OCD symptoms by affecting the serotonin system help these animals stop their pathological grooming.

Humans, too, engage in fixed action patterns, but we have a thinking "free will" part of our brain that interferes with the instinctual impulses, usually giving us considerable control over our primitive behavior patterns. But OCD rituals—scanning for danger, fear of contamination—can be seen as fixed action patterns run amok. My obsession with everything being "just so" may be a pathological concern with territorial order. From an evolutionary standpoint, it makes sense to scan the environment for potential danger, germs, and contamination, especially when protecting offspring. This may be why pregnancy can trigger or exacerbate OCD symptoms, causing women to become obsessed with contamination, intruders, or the possibility of harm coming to their babies.

A reptile's brain is basically just a limbic system that serves to mediate primitive drives. In higher animals, however, with the passing of millions and millions of years, the neocortex developed and enlarged. In humans, this newer part of the brain system is involved in regulating or "putting the brakes on" the primitive drives coming from the limbic system. In people with OCD, it may be that the neocortex is overreacting to these primitive drives of hygiene, territorial order, sex, and aggression, sending out so many inhibitory impulses that the OCD sufferer feels as though he or she is in constant danger and must take action, repeatedly, against that danger.

Looking at it this way, OCD is just an exaggerated version of perfectly normal human behavior. Some researchers think that people develop OCD because, for whatever reason, they become far too upset when they have a completely normal obsessive thought. "This is a horrible thought," they think, "I can't have these thoughts. I'm a terrible person because I have them. I have to do something in order to neutralize them."

Almost everyone—people who never have and never will suffer a day of OCD in their lives—has had to run back home to make sure they really turned off the stove. Almost everybody doodles. Many people throw salt over their shoulder to ward off bad luck. I've heard from "non OCDers" that they sometimes feel a sudden urge to veer the car off the road or that they tell themselves, "If I make this sequence of green lights, everything I'm worried about will be fine." People have lucky numbers. Non-OCD friends tell me that they sometimes trace letters on their hands with their index fingers, or flex their fingers as they imagine typing words into a computer keyboard—classic OCD "tracing" compulsions. It has been comforting for me to discover that my OCD oddities are really just exaggerations of "normal" behavior.

What separates normal obsessive thoughts and compulsive

rituals from full-blown OCD? The answer is: severity. You'll remember that in order to be considered OCD, obsessions and compulsions must cause a person distress, must be time-consuming, and must interfere with his or her functioning. This is what began to happen to me in my adolescence, which we'll explore in the next chapter.

To give you an idea of the types of obsessions and compulsions suffered by people with OCD, I've included a list of some of the most common OCD symptoms. Following that is the scale most commonly used by psychiatrists to evaluate the severity of obsessions and compulsions. It can serve as a gauge to get a sense of whether you have OCD and give you a clear idea of what's meant by "distress" and "interference with functioning." This test, Dr. Hollander cautions, does not replace a qualified doctor's diagnosis.

Yale-Brown
Obsessive Compulsive Checklist

OBSESSIONS

Aggressive Obsessions
- fear of harming self
- fear of harming others
- violent or horrific images
- fear of blurting out obscenities or insults

- fear of doing something else embarrassing
- fear of acting on unwanted impulses (e.g., stabbing a friend)
- fear of stealing something
- fear of harming others through carelessness (e.g., hit and run)
- fear of being responsible for something terrible (e.g., death of relative, fire)

Contamination Obsessions
- excessive concern or disgust with body wastes or secretions
- excessive concern with dirt or germs
- excessive concern with environmental contaminants (e.g., asbestos, radiation, toxic waste)
- excessive concern with household items (e.g., cleansers, solvents)
- excessive concern with animals (e.g., insects)
- excessive disgust with sticky substances or residues

Sexual Obsessions
- forbidden or perverse sexual thoughts, images, or impulses

Hoarding or Saving Obsessions
- excessive need to hoard or save "useless" items (as distinguished from wanting to save items as a "hobby," or because items have monetary or sentimental value)

Religious Obsessions
- excessive concern with sacrilege and blasphemy
- excessive concern with right and wrong or morality

Obsession with Symmetry, Exactness, or Order

• accompanied by magical thinking (e.g., concern that mother will have an accident unless things are in the right place)

• not accompanied by magical thinking

Somatic Obsessions

• excessive concern with illness or disease

• excessive concern with body part or aspect of appearance (e.g., nose too large)

Miscellaneous Obsessions

• fear of saying certain things

• fear of not saying just the right thing

• fear of losing things

• intrusive non-violent images

• intrusive nonsense sounds, words, or music

• belief in lucky or unlucky numbers

• belief in colors with special significance

COMPULSIONS

Cleaning and Washing Compulsions

• excessive or ritualized hand washing

• excessive or ritualized showering, bathing, tooth brushing, grooming, or toilet routine

• excessive cleaning of household items or other inanimate objects

Checking Compulsions

- checking locks, stove, appliances, etc.
- checking that one has not harmed or will not harm others
- checking that one has not harmed or will not harm self
- checking that nothing terrible has happened or will happen
- checking that one has not made a mistake

Repeating Rituals

- excessive rereading or rewriting
- repeating routine activities (e.g., repeatedly going in and out of house, repeatedly standing up and sitting down, etc.)
- stepping on cracks in sidewalk, or avoiding cracks in sidewalk

Counting Compulsions

- having to count over and over to a certain number

Ordering/Arranging Compulsions

- repeatedly packing and unpacking a suitcase, rearranging drawers
- repeatedly cleaning room
- excessively arranging items (e.g., food items alphabetically, closet by color or function)

Hoarding/Collecting Compulsions

- excessively saving old newspapers, mail, "useless" items (as distinguished from saving items as a "hobby," or because items have monetary or sentimental value)

Miscellaneous Compulsions
- excessive list making
- need to tell, ask, or confess
- need to touch, tap, or rub (e.g., touching moldings, tapping door frames)
- rituals involving blinking or staring
- ritualized eating behaviors
- self-damaging or self-mutilating behaviors

Yale-Brown
Obsessive Compulsive Scale

OBSESSIONS

1. How much of your time is occupied by obsessive thoughts? How frequently do the obsessive thoughts occur?

    0 = None.

    1 = Less than 1 hour per day, or occasional intrusions (occur not more than 8 times a day).

    2 = 1 to 3 hours per day, or frequent intrusions (occur more than 8 times a day, but most hours of the day are free of obsessions).

    3 = More than 3 and up to 8 hours per day, or very frequent intrusions.

    4 = More than 8 hours per day, or near-constant intrusions.

2. How much do your obsessive thoughts interfere with your work, school, social, or other important role functioning? Is there anything you don't do because of them?

> 0 = None.
>
> 1 = Slight interference with social or other activities, but overall performance not impaired.
>
> 2 = Definite interference with social or occupational performance, but still manageable.
>
> 3 = Causes substantial impairment in social or occupational performance.
>
> 4 = Incapacitating.

3. How much distress do your obsessions cause you?

> 0 = None.
>
> 1 = Mild, infrequent, and not too disturbing distress.
>
> 2 = Moderate, frequent, and disturbing distress, but still manageable.
>
> 3 = Severe, very frequent, and very disturbing distress.
>
> 4 = Extreme, near-constant, and disabling distress.

4. How much of an effort do you make to resist the obsessive thoughts? How often do you try to turn your attention away from these thoughts as they enter your mind?

> 0 = Try to resist all the time (or the symptoms are so minimal that there is no need to actively resist them).
>
> 1 = Try to resist most of the time.
>
> 2 = Make some effort to resist.

3 = Yield to all obsessions without attempting to control them, but I do so with some reluctance.

4 = Completely and willingly give in to all obsessions.

5. How much control do you have over your obsessive thoughts? How successful are you in stopping or diverting your obsessive thinking? (Note: Do not include here obsessions stopped by doing compulsions.)

0 = Complete control

1 = Usually able to stop or divert obsessions with some effort and concentration.

2 = Sometimes able to stop or divert obsessions.

3 = Rarely successful in stopping obsessions, can only divert attention with difficulty.

4 = Obsessions are completely involuntary, rarely able even momentarily to alter obsessive thinking.

COMPULSIONS

6. How much time do you spend performing compulsive behaviors? How much longer than most people does it take to complete routine activities because of your rituals? How frequently do you perform rituals?

0 = None.

1 = Less than 1 hour per day, or occasional performance of compulsive behaviors (occur not more than 8 times a day).

2 = 1 to 3 hours per day, or frequent performance of compulsive behaviors (more than 8 times a day, but most hours of the day are free of compulsions).

3 = More than 3 and up to 8 hours per day, or very frequent performance of compulsive behaviors.

4 = More than 8 hours per day, or near-constant performance of compulsive behaviors.

7. How much do your compulsive behaviors interfere with your work, school, social, or other important role functioning? Is there anything you don't do because of them?

0 = None.

1 = Slight interference with social or other activities, but overall performance not impaired.

2 = Definite interference with social or occupational performance, but still manageable.

3 = Causes substantial impairment in social or occupational performance.

4 = Incapacitating.

8. How would you feel if prevented from performing your compulsion(s)? How anxious would you become?

0 = Not at all anxious.

1 = Only slightly anxious if compulsions prevented.

2 = Anxiety would mount but remain manageable if compulsions prevented.

3 = Prominent and very disturbing increase in anxiety if compulsions interrupted.

4 = Incapacitating anxiety from any intervention aimed at reducing compulsions.

9. How much of an effort do you make to resist the compulsions?

0 = Try to resist all the time (or the symptoms are so minimal that there is no need to actively resist them).

1 = Try to resist most of the time.

2 = Make some effort to resist.

3 = Yield to almost all compulsions without attempting to control them, but I do so with some reluctance.

4 = Completely and willingly give in to all compulsions.

10. How strong is the drive to perform the compulsive behavior? How much control do you have over the compulsions?

0 = Complete control.

1 = Feel pressure to perform the compulsive behavior, but usually able to exercise voluntary control over it.

2 = Feel strong pressure to perform the compulsive behavior, can control it only with difficulty.

3 = Feel very strong drive to perform compulsive behavior, must be carried to completion, can only delay with difficulty.

4 = Drive to perform compulsive behavior experienced as completely involuntary and overpowering; rarely able even momentarily to delay activity.

Add up your scores on questions 1 through 10. A score above 8 can indicate mild OCD. Most people receiving treatment for OCD score between 20 and 30.

| *four* |

adolescent ambition,
adolescent angst

Aside from playing the trombone in our school band, in my teens, performing magic was the closest I could get to show business. I was desperate to perform, but I had no apparent talent. I wasn't funny, my singing sucked, and I couldn't dance. I had heard that television and film honchos like Johnny Carson and Orson Wells got their start as magicians, so I decided to give it a whirl.

But part of my obsessive compulsive condition is that for me nothing is ever casual: it's all or nothing. Once I commit that's it. I was determined to be the best kid magician in Indianapolis.

There was something about magic that hooked me: the ritualistic aspect of it, practicing the same trick over and over until it worked seamlessly, smoothly. Nothing in my hand and nothing up my sleeve. There was a cleanness, neatness, and precision about being a magician that gave me the same satisfaction I derived from my Sunday cleaning stints.

But the primary reason I liked magic was that it gave me a chance to perform. To stand up in front of people. To enthrall, entertain, and be the center of attention. I had a friend down the street, David Lawton, an accomplished magician, who helped build my show. I'd trot over to Dave's every night after dinner and pressure him into teaching me new tricks. By the time I was 12, I had my own act. Johnny called himself the great Carsoni, but I could never think of a moniker that rang right. I billed myself as Marc the Magician. It was the best I could come up with.

For $25 to $100 a pop I would perform at birthday parties. I practiced constantly, spending hours with a deck of cards or rolling coins over my fingers.

While I was doing so well at magic, however, something odd was happening to me academically. I had always been a good student, but I began to find studying increasingly difficult. My grades dropped. I lost the ability to concentrate on the written page. I found myself rereading the same paragraph twenty or thirty times, making sure I hadn't missed any words. I couldn't stop myself. I had no idea why. My lack of concentration made me frustrated and angry. I would stop trying to read and would roam around the house, trying to distract myself. I'd watch TV, get something to eat, talk to whoever was around. I *never* told my family or friends how I was feeling, what was happening to me. I thought maybe something was really wrong. "Why do I have to keep doing this?" I'd think to myself. "I must really be crazy." That's what happens to people who don't realize they have OCD—we figure we must be insane. It's terrifying. Although I later learned that my behaviors were typical of my OCD subgroup, at the time it was a nightmare. We have to do whatever it is that we do over and over until it's perfect, whether it's reading and rereading a passage or tying and retying our shoelaces until the loops are precisely the same size.

Professional pianists apparently have high rates of OCD. What distinguishes the professional pianist from the amateur is practice: the willingness, drive, or compulsion to play the same piece of music over and over. As Dr. Hollander has explained to me, in OCD sufferers these habitual routines form habit memory circuits in the basal ganglia of the brain. These circuits, while developed specifically for a piece of music or a series of ritualized actions to perform a magic trick, can generalize to other areas in the brain, broadening their application beyond their original purpose. Habitual actions loop in the brains of OCD sufferers like me. When the irrational fears that consume us don't actualize, we are convinced that we staved off whatever we were afraid of with our rituals, which reinforces our compulsion to do the habitual action. A vicious circle.

Grades were extremely important to me, as they are to many obsessive compulsive sufferers. We need things to be perfect, and we feel overwhelming anxiety if we don't live up to the strict guidelines we set for ourselves, whether it be checking a light switch 17 times or getting straight As. But, unlike your average perfectionist, I felt compelled to get good grades in order to allay feelings of unease and dread—in the same way I felt compelled to complete any one of my countless rituals to allay those same fears.

So I was deeply disturbed when my grades started to slide. By my sophomore year in high school, I had dropped to C-student level. My parents were completely unconcerned. Grades just weren't important to them. Unlike many of my friends, I was never praised or admonished for a report card. I had the only Jewish parents I knew who didn't push their kids to get into an Ivy League school. All the pressure I felt to be perfect I put on myself. Or, rather, OCD put the pressure on me.

One of my problems was that I couldn't turn in homework that had even a slight flaw—a smudge or eraser mark compelled me to redo the entire assignment. Standardized tests were hell. There was the stern warning, "Be sure you understand the directions before attempting to answer any questions." Great. I had to read the directions perfectly—my biggest nightmare. I'd get bogged down reading and rereading certain sentences and paragraphs of instructions. Then there was the announcement: "If you change an answer, be sure that all previous marks are erased completely. Incomplete erasures may be read as intended answers." It was a recipe for disaster. Heaven forbid I had to change an answer: I'd put a hole in the paper trying to erase it. Then I'd go nuts because you couldn't ask for another answer sheet. I'd have to live with that hole for the rest of the test.

I was disturbed by my inability to study and my academic performance, but the anxiety I felt about my grades was soon buried under my "obsession" with show business.

People use the term "obsession" all the time to refer to everything from their love of chocolate to their desire to rush home and watch *Dateline*, so let me explain what I mean. Technically, to qualify as an obsession in the OCD sense, a thought must be repetitive, intrusive, and unpleasant, and must interfere with one's life. My "obsession" with show business, therefore, was not a true obsession, but I've often felt there was something unnatural about it. Looking back, my instinct tells me that the intensity of my desire to perform, to enter the industry, was somehow related to my OCD.

I recently asked Dr. Hollander if he thought the two were related. Traditionally, OCD literature has firmly differentiated OCD, whose compulsions are never inherently pleasurable, from "pleasure seeking" compulsive disorders—compulsive gambling, compulsive shopping, binge eating disorders, and compulsive sexual addictions, which are all about pleasure gratification. Dr. Hollander, however, believes all these disorders are linked. They all have a common theme: it's hard for the sufferer to put brakes on the repetitive behaviors; we all have an excruciatingly hard time inhibiting or delaying acting on our impulses.

Dr. Hollander is currently investigating neurochemical links between OCD and the "pleasure gratification" disorders—it appears that they are all related to malfunctions in the same parts of the brain. So, according to Dr. Hollander, my tendency to fixate on pleasurable things—the elaborate fantasies I had as a kid about my future successes, my "obsession" with show business, my becoming determined to marry my future wife after laying eyes on her just once, my single-minded pursuit of my career—are all somehow related to my OCD. Which is not to say that everyone who ever fixates on a woman has OCD, but rather that, as an obsessive compulsive sufferer, my fixations and "obsessions" have an OCD-like quality—the same malfunctions in my brain that bring on my OCD also contribute to the intensity of my fixations.

Despite my academic woes, I felt hopeful about the future as long as I could watch Johnny Carson, Ed Sullivan, Steve Allen, Hollywood Palace, anything with *variety*. Variety is a television format you just don't see anymore. Variety shows came out of the great American traditions of vaudeville and burlesque, where anything could happen and anyone could perform: jugglers, clowns, dancing dogs, corny musical acts, slapstick comedy, the shtick meisters, the most ridiculous, outlandish talent was all paraded out onstage. You never knew when someone would crack you up, fall flat on his face, or capture your heart. So variety shows made for nervy, spontaneous TV. Talk shows have taken over this role today—the edginess, the unpredictability, the risk. But talk, with the exception of *The Jerry Springer Show*, doesn't quite have the zaniness of variety.

Age 13 was a big year for me. Dad lost Berkys Supermarket when Indiana University bought up the neighborhood. He was a nervous wreck. He picked himself up, though—went back to college, studied insurance, and became enormously successful: the vice president of the largest independent insurance agency in the state. But in the dawning of my manhood, that moment when the rug was pulled out from under my father's feet provided me with an acute sense of the fragility of life. Later on, when my career was hanging by a thread, when I felt my life was in shambles, I remembered my father's perseverance. His tenacity and grit were an inspiration to me.

I was bar mitzvahed on November 7, 1964. I had studied long and hard for the moment when I was called before the Torah. My rabbi, Maurice Davis, brought me close to religion. He didn't lecture to our Sunday school class; he talked to us as peers. When I studied for my bar mitzvah, Rabbi Davis was in his early fifties, a balding, gray-haired, distinguished man who always wore bow ties. His eyes were dark, deep, and full of humor. To me, they looked like he spoke to God daily.

My grandfather had studied to be a rabbi and had high expectations for my bar mitzvah, so I worked extra-hard to get the prayers right. Our synagogue was the ultra-reform Indianapolis Hebrew Congregation, located in an upper-middle-class neighborhood. In my comedy routines, I joked that there was a cross over the pulpit. It was the most modern temple in town. The rabbi pressed a button and the doors of the ark swung open to reveal the Torah. We had a huge choir. The place felt like magic—like showbiz.

I was particularly taken with the way Rabbi Davis orchestrated the proceedings on the day of my bar mitzvah. He seemed to have so much power, so much assurance. He was completely in control of the event. And yet there was no aggression about it. It was as if he had effortlessly picked up the congregation and was piloting us through sacred realms. And then he handed the controls to me. I was nervous and excited, filled with wonder and a deep sense of awe.

After that, I wanted to become a rabbi. What is a rabbi if not a performer? I wanted to be able to create the feeling in the room that Rabbi Davis engendered. That safe, enclosed space of ritual and magic. I know it sounds silly, but I think there are parallels between being a television show host and being a rabbi. Both professionals speak to, affirm, even define a community. Both have their prescribed sets of actions that have been determined beforehand, rituals reenacted at set times. Both the temple and the television studio are spaces separated from our everyday world.

After my bar mitzvah, I obsessed on my performance. The temple had recorded an audiotape of my speech and prayers, and I played it over and over, listening to each nuance in my intonation, imagining myself standing up in front of my friends and family, relishing how I looked in my black suit and tie, rekindling the attention and admiration that had flowed toward me from the audience.

My brief moment of glory in the synagogue redoubled my ambition to be a performer. I fantasized endlessly about playing *The Tonight Show*, the *crème de la crème* of television. Johnny Carson blew me away. He was hip and clever. Anyone who was anyone made an appearance on his show: Sinatra, Streisand, Woody Allen. Carson was topical. He spoke to what was going on in the nation. He brought the country together and made us feel like we were all privy to an enormous inside joke, and that we all participated in an endlessly weird, eternally fascinating, patently ridiculous yet somehow moving comedy of this country. He hooked me.

When I was 14, Rabbi Davis took our Sunday school class on a trek to New York City. In those days, *The Tonight Show* was taped at NBC Studios at 30 Rockefeller Plaza in Manhattan.

Some people say the show changed when it moved to L.A. I think that the L.A. shows were first-rate television, but in New York, Carson had that vaudeville feel. Ethel Merman, for instance, would come in and sing a song from her Broadway show.

When we went to New York, I was determined to break into national television in a big way. I would appear with Johnny on *The Tonight Show*, I thought. Having read *The Tonight Show* credits hundreds of times, I knew that the talent coordinator— and my contact to Carson—was Mike Zanella. I'd simply call Mr. Zanella and convince him that it would be supremely cool to have a 14-year-old magician from the Midwest on the show. If he balked, I'd remind him that his boss had started out as a magician from Nebraska (Johnny got his start in television doing *Carson Cellar*, a show for a CBS L.A. affiliate called KNXT, and as a writer for Red Skelton. Johnny got his big break in the late 1950s, when Red injured himself falling through a trap door. Johnny filled in for Red, and the rest is history.)

Typical of star-struck teens and OCD sufferers alike, I ran elaborate, repetitive fantasies in my mind. Johnny would dust off old tricks, and we would have a battle of the Midwest magicians. He would jump at the chance.

A month before our class trip, I began calling Mr. Zanella. I called him early in the morning, during my lunch break, and late in the day when I came home from school. He was always in meetings, prepping with Johnny for a show, out to lunch. He would get back to me, his secretary said. (At the time, I didn't realize that this was a perfect foreshadowing of things to come in L.A.)

My parents didn't know how focused I was on Zanella. I

called him on my private phone line. How, you might ask, was a 14-year-old able to afford a private line? I think my OCD was at least partially responsible. I had asked for my own phone.

"Fine!" my parents said. "You want a phone? You pay for it."

And I did. My savings account was flush from performing my magic shows, my paper route, lawn cutting, and other odd jobs. I had a sterling reputation. I was absolutely dependable. People knew I always showed up. I was always on time. I never made a mess.

At 6:30 one evening I made my obligatory call to Zanella. The voice on the line wasn't his secretary's.

"Marc Summers for Mr. Zanella," I said.

"This is Mike."

Zanella had actually picked up his phone! This was my chance. I made my pitch. Me. Johnny. Magic. The Midwest. I told him when I would be in New York and gave him the hotel's phone number. He was cordial. He'd discuss the idea with Johnny and get back to me.

When I arrived in New York, there was no message from Zanella. I checked the front desk every ten seconds. I saw my first Broadway play, *Fiddler on the Roof,* which I loved; went to the Statue of Liberty; searched for my Jewish roots in Williamsburg, Brooklyn. On my next-to-last day in the city, I frantically phoned Zanella to remind him that I was in town for another 24 hours. I would have to do the program that evening. Period.

He didn't return my call.

I was crestfallen, but I had the one trait essential to show business: never, ever give up. Take your licks and keep on coming. Looking back, my OCD-related traits—my uncompromising pursuit of perfection and my insistence on following through on everything I started—helped me achieve my goals. I had my eyes fixed on the prize. No disappointments, even at the hands of the likes of Mike Zanella, could shake me loose.

At 15 and 16 years old, I was torn between the rabbinate and the life of a TV broadcaster. Coincidentally, there was an assistant rabbi at our synagogue, Mr. Weitzman, who had majored in radio and television back in his pre-rabbi days.

When I was 16, I went to him for advice. He was a short man and wore glasses with thick black frames. His impish grin made him seem playful and approachable.

"What should I do with my life?" I asked him.

"What do you want to do?"

"Part of me wants to be a rabbi, and part of me wants to go into show business."

He closed his eyes and stroked his chin with his thumb and forefinger. "Why do you want to be a rabbi?" he asked.

"Because I want to help people."

"Well, as a rabbi you help a few people a lot. In show business, you help a lot of people a little."

I pondered his words, and opted for show business. But to this day I often wonder what my life would have been like had I decided to immerse myself in the Torah. Through my work with the Obsessive Compulsive Foundation I've had a chance to reach out and help people in a direct way, to make a difference in their lives. This is what I had hoped for as a teenager when I dreamed of being a rabbi. I hope I can, in this book, be something like a rabbi, someone people in distress can go to for guidance and help in making their way in the world.

In ninth grade, the intrusive thoughts of harm coming to my parents diminished. I no longer had that awful step-on-a-crack-break-my-mother's-back feeling (the person who thought up *that* ditty definitely had OCD). I no longer thought that if I didn't nail a test or do everything perfectly my parents would die.

But other intrusive thoughts didn't stop: they continued to plague me. It seems that many kids outgrow obsessive thoughts of causing their parents harm, but they develop other obsessions in their teenage years. My obsessions were multiple and omnipresent. I was obsessed with symmetry, order, neatness, and cleanliness. I was obsessed with the state of my room, the state of my clothes, the state of my homework, and with the countless rituals that filled my days. (Not all OCs are like this. Some people with OCD are focused on only one thing—keeping their personal appearance immaculate, for example. Most people with single-obsession OCD are probably undiagnosed and untreated because their symptoms are usually not as debilitating as multiply obsessed OCs.)

In adolescence, my obsessive anxieties with my parents' mortality branched out into a vast arena of placating and propitiating ritual. If I didn't put on my baseball uniform in a certain way (stirrup socks, then white socks, both pant legs pulled down evenly), I'd be tagged out at third base. If I didn't repeat a line just right, I'd forget it onstage. If I didn't check my magic props

15 times, I'd flub my gig. I turned everything into a ritual to appease some god of ill fortune who scrutinized my every move.

Checking magic props is something all good magicians do. There's no room for sloppiness in magic. For master magician Lance Burton, repetitive prop checking is probably just superstition. But my compulsion to check props was OCD related, as was my flirtation with the religious life. There's an interesting relationship between ritual, magic, superstition, and religion.

The ultimate goal of religion is to deal with fear of the unknown, fear of uncertainty, the doubt that comes from being born into a vast, largely incomprehensible universe. Religion uses ritual to lessen those fears in just the way an OCD sufferer uses magical and superstitious thinking to alleviate anxieties. My devotion to magic through my high school years was, I think, partially because magic was largely about practicing ritual. And being a magician allowed me to enter a realm where I was in control of what the world perceived as unseen forces, even if I knew it was all in the props. It's ironic that as an OCD sufferer I believed in magic even though as a magician I knew it was all smoke and mirrors.

In 1970, I graduated from high school. I was embarrassed about my mediocre class ranking since many of my friends were hotshot students, but my parents weren't concerned. Dad wanted a partner in the insurance business. "You'll be great with sales," he said. But I loathed the thought of working 9 to 5, stuck in an office all day. Show business was the life for me.

I thought I could make a career appearing on radio and TV that was aimed at and run for the armed services. Since the military's neatness and regimentation appealed to me, I enlisted in the navy. I was thrown out during basic training for bad knees, however, and I arrived home, deflated and beaten. My friends were away in college, and I had no idea what I was going to do next.

I haunted Indianapolis' radio and TV stations, futilely searching for work. No one would hire me, but broadcasting was the only thing I was truly interested in. I lay around the house all day watching TV, until my father set me up with a job in the commercial loan department of a local bank.

Stressed out about not being able to break into broadcasting, I would have chest pains every afternoon at the bank. My blood pressure was off the charts. "What's the matter with you?" said the doctor the bank brought in to check out its employees. "You'll be dead before you're 30 if you don't do something about this!"

I was 18.

Mom clipped an add from *Seventeen* magazine: "Come to Boston—learn radio and television at Grahm Junior College."

"Why don't you check it out?" she said.

I still have that little scrap of paper.

I interviewed at the college, staying with Rhonda, a high school friend who lived in an all-girls' dorm. The thrill of it! I was still a virgin, and when I woke up in the dorm room, Rhonda's roommate was stark naked, combing her long, dark hair. Boston was the place for me!

That school was just what I needed. I was a DJ at the college radio station and a host on the college television station. I learned that illustrious alumni had preceded me. The future creator of *Alf*, Paul Fusco, and Burt Dubrow, Executive Producer of *Sally*

Jessy Raphael and *Jerry Springer*, had gone to Grahm. So had co-median Andy Kaufman. Everybody at Grahm wanted to work in the industry. We saw the school as a fast track to work. Grahm had real television studios and a real radio station. "Learn by Doing" was the school's motto. That was fine by me.

My compulsion for neatness didn't wane once I began living in a dorm. One night, a classmate came into my room and threw a wad of paper in the wastebasket. He talked to me for a few minutes, then left.

I didn't use wastebaskets. Ever. I couldn't stand the thought of garbage piling up in my room, even in a contained basket.

In school, if I had to throw something out, I'd march into the hall and deposit it into the communal garbage can. The guys in the dorm knew this, and they hid in the hall to see how long it would take me to empty my trash. Immediately after my class-mate left, I walked out with the basket. All the guys laughed at me. I didn't like the laughter but I knew I couldn't control the compulsion.

As they snickered and guffawed, it was driven home to me that I was different. My dorm-mates were all inveterate slobs, their beds full of ancient pizza slices, their floors covered with filthy socks and underwear. I had to ask myself: why wasn't I a slob like a normal 18-year-old boy?

"Okay, you guys," I said. "I got it. You caught me." I was lucky that I had enough self-esteem not to be thrown by their teasing. But other teenagers aren't as fortunate. Many young people with OCD think they're crazy. They feel disturbed, even disgusted, by their obsessive thoughts and are too humiliated to seek help. They're lost in teenage angst.

I've traveled around the country hosting community discussions on OCD, and I've met countless teens with the disorder, and their parents. After talking with them I realize the most important thing is that parents recognize the pressures on their teenagers. It's tough out there! Teens need to forge relationships in a highly competitive social world. They face enormous peer pressure and they feel the need to conform. And to have OCD on top of that? Ouch! The parents who do best both for their children and for themselves make an effort to educate themselves through reading about OCD. They remember that OCD is not a character flaw but a treatable medical condition.

I doubt my college roommate Mike viewed my cleaning compulsion as a character flaw. He certainly benefited from it. Each Thursday the school issued clean sheets and towels. Thursday evenings I'd throw Mike out and clean the room, top to bottom. I *needed* to do it. It would have been torture for me, so intense would have been the physical discomfort, if I had not been able to clean the room from 7:30 P.M. until 11:00. Mike considered himself a lucky guy: he had a roommate with a bizarre eagerness to clean. What can I say, Mike? I was a classic case.

I sojourned in Beantown the summer before my sophomore year, living in a Brighton apartment with the two biggest pigs in the world. They couldn't stand me, and I couldn't stand them. The place was in total disarray all the time; the kitchen was a filthy, disgusting mess. There was so much grease in our oven that it would catch fire twice a week. I never ate a meal there; I *always* ate out. My high school sweetheart, Ann, once came to stay with me for a week. Before she arrived I cleaned madly, moving couches, dusting, Pledging, vacuuming. There was enough hair on the bathroom floor to fashion a full body suit for a gorilla. For a brief moment that apartment smelled the way my room at home smelled every Sunday evening.

Before the school year started again, I marched into Grahm's Director of Housing's office and demanded my own room. It was against college policy, the director informed me. I threw a fit: "I've tried living in doubles! I need to live alone! I need a single!"

He must have sensed I was absolutely determined, because he gave me what I wanted. I loved my single. It was the cleanest dorm room in Boston.

| *five* |

waiting at the altar

What happens when someone with OCD is left waiting at the altar? I'll tell you, he goes berserk.

Alice, my wife-to-be, was nearly an hour late for the wedding photos that were supposed to be taken before our marriage ceremony. I had arrived early, of course, at the temple in Westchester, an L.A. suburb, where we were to be married. My mother, father, sister, and brother were there. The photographer was there. The rabbi was there. The wedding party was there. The 250 guests had begun to gather. But Alice was nowhere to be found. And neither was her family.

The day was Sunday, June 16, 1974, and I was losing it, pacing and fuming.

"Where is she? Where is she?" I kept muttering. "I can't believe she's doing this!"

Think of a "normal" person's anxiety in such a situation, and then multiply it by a million. That was me. People with OCD are adversely affected by stress. Our symptoms tend to become more pronounced. And for my subgroup of obsessive compulsives—in addition to my need for neatness, I'm also a punctuality freak—lateness on one's wedding day was a capital crime. No punishment was too severe.

I couldn't stop looking at the clock. "I cannot believe this!" I was wound tight as watch. I kept storming outside, looking up and down the street.

Finally, finally they came.

I dashed toward Alice. "Jesus! Where have you been?" I grabbed her and hustled her inside. "What on earth happened?"

Instead of being a supportive, understanding future husband, I was a screaming maniac.

Alice was furious. "What's wrong with you? We're a little late. That's all."

We were screaming at each other right there in temple, in public. I remember my mother telling me to calm down, but I couldn't.

"Mom! You talk to her!"

"She's your wife," my mother retorted.

In the wedding pictures, you can tell Alice was furious.

I felt no guilt. In my mind, my anger was completely justified. "How *dare* she arrive late?" I later learned that she and her parents had been trying to clean off nail polish that had spilled on her mother's dress. I was unmoved. "Well," I thought, "what a ridiculous thing to have done. They shouldn't have spilled that polish. They should have been more careful. They should have planned ahead." There was no excuse, ever, for lateness.

Nevertheless, I must have eventually apologized, because the wedding was terrific.

I still fume to myself when people are late. It's a horrible corrosive monologue that repeats and repeats in my head. I associate that kind of explosive anger with OCD. It makes no sense to me that people wouldn't show up on time. Why wouldn't they? I assume everyone lives his life the way I live mine. And my life runs with such precision that I'm never late. For me, there's no excuse for being late, short of being dead.

Funny that I should work in Hollywood, where big-shots keep you waiting intentionally. They play mind games with time. It makes me so sad: you look like an idiot, sitting there, hanging out with the receptionist while the boss chats on the phone, files his nails, and does whatever other meaningless tasks he's doing. I won't wait more than 30 minutes for a meeting. It's partly OCD-induced irritation, partly business sense. You start to lose credibility if you've been sitting around for an hour and the guy you're waiting on finally calls in on his cellular to let his receptionist know he's just leaving his lunch date. If you think I'm pigheaded, I have friends in the industry who won't wait more than 15 minutes.

Alice and I had wanted to leave on our honeymoon that night, but I had a run-through the next day for a show. I had recently met Marty Pasetta, then the hottest television producer-director in Hollywood. He wanted to get into game shows and brought me in as part of the talent team for a pilot we were pitching to the networks titled *Discover America*. We were due for a final run-through the day after the wedding in front of network executives to see if they wanted the show. Alice understood this was a big chance for me. If the show had gone (it didn't) it would have been a big boost to my career. The chance to work with the hottest guy in town was what I'd been pushing toward since I graduated from college the previous May.

After graduation, I'd had two choices: L.A. or New York. I was a die-hard television person, and for die-hard television people, there are just two cities in the whole world. At the time, my brother was living in L.A., playing drums for Helen Reddy ("I am woman, hear me roar . . ."). He said I could stay with him. My decision was made: I left Boston and headed for L.A.

The previous winter break I had been out visiting my brother and had fallen into conversation with his next-door neighbor. The guy said he could get me into the Director's Guild Apprentice Program. The Director's Guild is the hardest Hollywood union to get into. You almost have to be born into it. Thousands of people apply to the apprentice program each year: you have to take a long test, and then a lucky 25 are accepted. Just 25 each year! Being accepted into the DGAP is basically a license to work the rest of your life, assuming you don't do anything incredibly stupid. The Director's Guild opens doors to the industry, introducing you to key contacts, which is what the L.A. world is all about. Schmoozing and ingratiating yourself. Knowing the right people. Slowly, tenaciously clawing your way up the food chain.

Being in the Director's Guild Apprentice Program gets you assistantships on movies. Now, I wanted to work in television, and knew nothing about film. But I'd directed college TV, and I figured directing film and television were the same thing. (I've since learned they have nothing to do with each other.)

I was thrilled. It was all I talked about in my last semester of college—how I had this connection in L.A. who was going to get me into the DGAP.

Now, finally in L.A., I knocked on my brother's neighbor's door.

"Hi, remember me, Marc? I was visiting my brother? Last winter? You mentioned you could help get me into the DGAP?"

He didn't know what I was talking about. Denied ever having said anything about helping me. "Here's their address," he told me. "Go call them. And good luck."

To think I'd taken his promise to heart! Still in my Midwest mindset, back then I believed what anybody told me. "Indoctrination by fire" is what I think when I look back at the abuse I took in my early years in L.A.

I did go to the DGAP offices, though, down on Beverly Boulevard. They were filled with white leather couches and palm trees. I managed to convince a secretary to get me into a lower-level executive's office, but the guy had no time for me and told me to get lost.

I had one more lead: Michael Zinberg, the associate producer of the original *Mary Tyler Moore Show* and *The Bob Newhart Show.* These were major hits, which made him a hotshot.

I called. "Hi, you don't know me but your brother just married my best friend's sister and I'm looking for a job."

He chuckled. "If you've got the guts to make this phone call, I've got to see you."

He told me he might have something for me. It turned out to be the important sounding job of "production assistant," aka gopher. A chance to be at some egomaniac's beck and call. To run around like a lunatic slave. In other words, this job was what every 20-year-old fresh out of Grahm Junior College dreamed of.

Zinberg invited me to come in and talk to him. I was on my way.

His office was in Studio City, a five-minute drive from North Hollywood where I was living at the time with my brother. Zinberg was in his late twenties, tall, tan, and blond, with a thick, reddish-blond mustache. He looked like he'd just stepped off the tennis court. A typical Hollywood hey-babe-let's-do-lunch kinda guy. He told me I was overqualified for the job, and I told him, thanks for the kind words but my being overqualified wasn't his decision to make, it was mine. "You're too smart," he said. "You're going to get bored, you're going to find something else to do, and you're going to leave us. I need someone who'll stick around for a while." I was mad but powerless.

He did have a friend, though, Bobby Roads, who was in charge of the pages at CBS. Pages bring honchos coffee, seat people in the studio, and give tours. They are the grunts of the industry, the first step into the business.

Eight years later, after I'd been around and climbed a few ladders, I asked Zinberg why he hadn't hired me for the job.

"Because you came across as the most arrogant, self-centered jerk I'd ever met in my life," he told me. Which, looking back, was kind of the way I was. I had always been taught that walking into a meeting with confidence impressed people. But I guess I took it too far.

Far from believing I had anything messed up in my head, I thought I was the "rightest" person in the world. Always on time, always correct, always neat—I wasn't odd, the rest of the world was sloppy, slow, and negligent.

I left Zinberg's office and made a beeline for CBS, which was 15 minutes away on Beverly Boulevard. CBS was a huge television factory with four enormous studio buildings. At that time, the network had a string of hits, including *The Price Is Right, Sonny and Cher,* and *All in the Family.*

Roads, a bottom-rung executive at CBS, was a scrawny, mousy fellow. His hair was always combed the wrong way. His face looked dried-out and pale, and his eyes were always darting around. He had a habit of constantly looking over your shoulder to see if there was somebody more important he should be talking to. He organized the weekly schedule for fifty or sixty pages every Monday morning. This was no small task, as many of the pages were still in school or working part-time. When I met him, he'd been at his position a year.

He gave me the same story Zinberg had—different job, but I was still overqualified. "I need pages who are going to be here for at least eighteen months," he said. "You're going to be here today, gone tomorrow." Well, of course, I thought. That's why people get jobs as pages—to move up. What I said was, "It's kind of you to say I'm overqualified, but I don't feel I am. I wouldn't be in this office if I didn't feel this job was the one for me."

No dice. Like Zinberg, in place of a job he gave me a lead. He'd heard that a new cable company (that was 1973, nobody knew what cable was back then) needed a production manager. I should give them a call.

I drove out to the cable company in Simi Valley. This was on the other side of the world from where I lived. I got lost, I had no idea where I was going. It took me nearly two hours to find the cinder block building that housed the company. The office was barren, no pictures on the walls. It exemplified the true meaning of the term "start-up." (Who knew at that time that cable was the future of the business? Everybody thought cable was a joke. The networks were God. Now, after being in the business for 25 years, I find it fascinating to watch the networks lose power as cable becomes king.)

I met with my contact and was hired right on the spot, as a production manager! It was a job beyond my wildest dreams, miles and miles above working as a production assistant. To think that I'd actually been eager to work that job! I was amazed, ecstatic. I was going to help run the production side of the company, and I'd be on the air part-time doing local news for Simi Valley. Experience on both sides of the camera, and good money to boot. It was a dream job. I drove the 30 miles back to CBS studios to thank Bobby Roads in person. I told him what a terrific job it was, and how grateful I was for the lead.

"Way to go," he congratulated me. "You nailed it!"

I was a kid from the Midwest; that was the right thing to do.

Two hours later, back at my brother's apartment, the phone rang. It was the person who hired me. "I'm sorry," he said. "I've had second thoughts. I can't use you."

I was flabbergasted. "What's changed in the two hours?"

It turned out that as soon as I'd left Roads' office, he'd picked up the phone and called the cable station.

"Mr. Roads is more qualified than you are," said my guy. "I had no choice but to hire him over you."

Bobby Roads had stolen my job! But he'd given me the lead!

I jumped in the car and flew straight back to Roads' office.

"How could you have done this?" I demanded.

Roads did feel guilty. Not guilty enough to say no to the job, but sufficiently guilty to offer me a post with CBS as a page. I was outraged, I wanted to kill him. But not so outraged that I didn't accept the page job.

The world of television was different in 1973. Without cable, there were only NBC, CBS, ABC, independent stations, and the syndication business. (These had independent producers and sold to local stations. Anybody could buy those shows, then as now.) There wasn't nearly as much work back then, and everybody wanted to work for a network. So, after my inauspicious beginning, I'd finally landed a job at CBS: the coolest of the cool, the Tiffany of all networks.

I began working as a page, the job for which I had been warned I was overqualified. I gave studio tours, ran messages to producers, took entrance tickets. If Carol Burnett said to me, "Excuse me, would you get me some coffee?" my job was to say, "Of course, Miss Burnett, would you like cream and sugar?" People were killing to get my job. I made $2.73 an hour, and I would have worked for free.

Bob Barker, the host of *Truth or Consequences* and *The Price Is Right*, was my role model. He was smooth, funny, and the nicest guy in the world. One day I dashed up to him as he was passing through the studio.

"I watched you every day when I came home from nursery school," I gushed.

His smile turned to a frown. This blunder was my first inkling of hyper age-consciousness in Hollywood and the pressure most celebrities feel after they reach a certain age. Back then, Barker would have called 39 "the dark year," but today I'd say the cut-off is more like 28, assuming you have spiked hair and an MTV look. If not, you're probably done for at 25.

Despite this dubious introduction, Barker and I went on to become friends. I modeled my career after his. We both idolized Jack Benny, whose stardom, we agreed, was due to his great generosity. Barker's theory, which became mine, was that if you make contestants look good, you, in turn, look good. Let your contestants and your guests get the laughs.

My best friend at CBS was a fellow page, Steve Weinberg. I was 21 and he was a little older, a wise man of 23 or 24. Steve was a hound: he used his post to pick up women. A smorgasbord of women were always lined up, waiting to get into the studio. He tried to get himself scheduled to work on *The Price Is Right*, since the women lined up for *The Price Is Right* were known throughout the page world as the cream of the crop. They were big-busted and came dressed to the nines, hoping to be chosen as contestants. So Steve would work the line, trying his luck: "Here's my card. I work for CBS." "Here's my card. I'll get you into the show." "Here's my card. I'll ask Bob to put you on . . ."

Television: for Steve, it was a great way to get a date. For me, it was my introduction to my bride-to-be.

A month into my new job, Steve and I were standing on the set of *The Mary Tyler Moore Show*. I glanced up at the line of people waiting to enter the studio for the taping of the day's episode, "Angels in the Snow." And then I saw her. At least on my end, the chemistry was instantaneous. She was about 5-foot-2, with long dark hair, dressed in an ankle-length skirt, knee-high boots, a thin silk top and dark jacket.

I leaned over to Steve: "That's the woman I'm going to marry."

"That's nice." He was skeptical. "But I think she's already engaged to a friend of mine."

Oh.

I watched my newfound mate (Alice was her name, Steve told me) file into her seat with her boyfriend. She looked like she was having the worst time of her life. Suddenly, she stood up and walked toward us. Unlike my buddy Steve, I was shy with girls. My pulse was racing, but I had to talk to her. Was it fate? She was right in front of me.

"Excuse me," she said. "Could you tell me where the bathroom is?"

Her words were poetry to my ears. "What's it worth to you?" I grinned.

She laughed, and I walked her to the bathroom. It was beautiful.

After the show, Alice and her guy hung around to chat. He was a fake-producer type. Turn over any stone in Hollywood and you'll find one with his own "production company." They whip out fancy business cards, but they've never worked in the industry. That was as true in 1973 as it is now. I could tell how miserable Alice was, but I'm not sure how I knew. Maybe it was the way she carried herself, the look on her face, the way she glanced up and around the room when her boyfriend was speaking.

When they left, I said to Steve, "Let me know when they break up." Steve shook his head and sighed. "Don't hold your breath."

A month later, Steve called to tell me Alice and her boyfriend had broken up. He agreed to call Alice, who remembered meeting me, albeit vaguely. Then I called Alice and asked her out. She said she'd be more comfortable if we double-dated with Steve.

So it was that we went out on a double date that night.

I knew just the place. An old Victorian castle in the Hollywood Hills called the Magic Castle Night Club. Celebrities walked around the club with drinks in their hands watching magic acts. People called it Disneyland for adults. Back then, nothing was bigger than the Magic Castle. You couldn't get in unless you knew somebody. Cary Grant was on the board of directors. To buy a club membership cost $1,000. They had 17 valet parkers running around outside to get you your car.

The Magic Castle Night Club is still around. The bloom is off the rose, however. Bill Larson, an executive at CBS who started the place and ran it in its heyday, died a few years ago. But a booking at the Magic Castle is still a huge event for a magician. And I had just landed a part-time job performing there, which made me a performing member. Which meant I could get us in. As a page, you saved up for dates; Steve and I had been saving for weeks for a night like this. Since I was out with the girl of my dreams, money was no object.

I remember the night like it was yesterday. The four of us strode up to the Castle. I was giddy. Alice held my arm. I gave the receptionist my name and she checked her list. My heart was pounding. She flipped pages for what seemed like an eternity. Finally, she nodded her head. We were in! Except, as we glided through the door, another host reached his arm out and barred Alice's way.

"ID, ma'am?" She looked 21 to me, but it turned out she was only 20. The host was sorry, but he couldn't let her in. They could lose their liquor license. I don't know who was more embarrassed, Alice or me. She'd been carded, but my vaunted clout hadn't pulled us through.

We ended up at a small restaurant in Beverly Hills for wine and as much free cheese as we could eat. Steve's date was Susan Bierfisher, a mature woman of 27 and a secretary in CBS's executive offices. The four of us wandered the streets of Westwood after our wine and cheese. We passed through a little arcade where people sold jewelry on the street. That's when I first kissed Alice. You have to understand, although I was outgoing, a ham, and lived to be on TV, I was desperately shy around girls. For me to ask a girl out was a major move. And to KISS a girl! Incredible. But everything was different with Alice. There was something special about her, a warm glow. Everything felt right. I was loose and able to open up and express my feelings.

Steve drove us back to the rendezvous point where I'd left my car. Alice lived with her folks, and I delivered her home at 1 A.M.

We kissed goodnight at her door. I was on cloud nine. I walked back to my green '68 Oldsmobile and cranked the key but it wouldn't start. It was completely dead. I swallowed my pride and knocked on her door.

She came out, laughed, and we drove around in her car at 2 A.M. looking for a gas station to get someone to come jump the car.

"We're going to look back at this and laugh," I told her.

"What are you talking about?"

"I'll tell you later," I smiled to myself. I was determined to marry her.

The next day I sent her a dozen long-stemmed red roses.

We dated five nights a week. I was very skinny then, and full of energy. I couldn't afford food: my page's salary was less than $350 a month, and I paid $125 in rent. After putting gas in the car, I could afford little else. I'd show up at *The Joker's Wild,* a daytime game show, an hour before call time, slip into the room where lunch was laid out for the contestants, and stuff my pockets with sandwiches. If a page got lucky, he or she would be assigned to a show over at the Studio Center in Studio City in the Valley, where they actually *fed* you lunch.

Five weeks after our first date I asked Alice to marry me. "You're crazy," she told me. "You don't even know me."

Two weeks later, in October, I asked her again. This time she said yes.

Until this point, Alice hadn't encountered my OCD symptoms, which didn't exhibit themselves on dates. She knew, of course, how focused I was on my work, and how fanatically punctual I was. I was a nut for being on time. Sometimes I'd arrive at

6:00 for a 7:00 date. I'd drive around the block for 15 minutes, and then say, ah, forget it, and go ring Alice's bell. She wouldn't be ready, and it frustrated her. But she accepted it. Better than having a perpetually late boyfriend, I suppose. And I guess she thought I was just incredibly eager to see her. Which I was.

But, of course, it was more than that. When Alice came to my apartment she saw it was neat, but in those days I was living in a tiny one-bedroom with a queen-size bed and a bookshelf that I'd made from plywood and bricks. There wasn't much to obsess over. So she was completely unprepared when I screamed at her on our wedding day for being late for the photo session.

After the wedding, which, despite my hysteria, was wonderful, as I've said—lots of dancing and toasting and the feeling of happiness, joy thick in the air, new beginnings, and our families embracing us in a circle of love and sending us out into the world, we went back to my little apartment, which was now our little apartment. Our wedding night was bliss. Alice seemed to have completely forgotten my outburst. I did my run-through the next day. When I came home, we started packing, getting ready to leave for our Hawaiian honeymoon.

Alice's red Amelia Earhart suitcase was sitting in a corner. She opened it, banging its top against the spanking white wall. I had the same response that I had had at our wedding. I started yelling, screaming, upbraiding her, telling her to be more careful, stomping around the room, throwing up my hands. She was completely baffled. She had no idea what had caused my explosion.

I didn't know if there was a scratch in the wall. If there was, it was certainly nothing a normal person would have noticed. The point was that Alice had banged the wall, and I hated that. Know-

ing that she had done it, I then had to go over and touch the spot
the suitcase had dinged. I had no idea why at the time, it was
something I'd been doing all my life. If I saw a mark on the wall,
I had to go touch it. It didn't make sense. It still doesn't. Today,
when I see a wall nicked or marred, I still have to keep putting
my hand on the damaged spot. I can't explain what goes on in my
head. It's not like I think I'm Oral Roberts and can heal the wall
with my hand. There's no logic to it. All I know is that for most of
my life the compulsion was so strong I never even considered trying to override it.

I was sarcastic, self-righteous, fuming. "Try to be a little more
careful, okay?" I remember saying. "Try not to bang the wall."

Finally, she realized what had set me off. It was her turn to ex-
plode. "The suitcase hit the wall! So what? What is the matter
with you?"

And somewhere I must have sensed how crazy I was because
I apologized. Alice had hurt feelings, but eventually we kissed,
made up, and had a terrific week in Hawaii.

Back at home we settled into domestic life. Alice's parents
bought us a new couch. Wedding money bought bookshelves. I
didn't have much of a wardrobe, but Alice, being a dental assistant, had actual outfits. We shared closet space. She had her side,
I had my side. There was a little partition down the middle.
Whatever she did on her side was fine, as long as it didn't touch
my side. Now don't get me wrong, Alice was (and still is) an incredibly neat and clean human being. But nobody, short of my father, could keep a closet the way I kept mine.

When I was promoted to head page, I got a small raise. My
salary was now $87 a week, and Alice took home about $100,

maybe $105 a week. (I recently found our first combined tax return out in the garage. I save everything. That first year, Alice made $9,000 and I made $4,000.) I worked as much overtime as was available, and on a good week I made $135. I also worked part-time doing warm-ups on *The Joker's Wild*. Shows with studio audiences often have someone warm the crowd up before filming begins, to get them so geared up, giddy, and giggly that they'll laugh at just about anything. I continued to work part-time at Magic Castle, which paid a measly $125 for seven straight nights, four shows a night. Even back then, that was highway robbery.

Alice didn't like The Magic Castle. Too many creepy people hanging around. Too many characters.

I worked sunup to sundown, going from job to job. I was driven to do any work at all in the industry. I ate, slept, and drank television. For me, L.A. was the best place to be in the world.

Alice and I were happy together. Show business wasn't important to her, but her attitude was "If he's happy, I'm happy." She let me go out and do my thing.

I was a hustler, trying to hustle up work. I still am, and I still try.

A year or two into our marriage I got a job for Hertz Rent A Car. They billed me as "The Great MIRAHCFU (May-I-Rent-A-Hertz-Car-For-You), the Magician." I stood in their booth at conventions dressed in a yellow brocade tuxedo and did magic tricks. The object was to draw people into the booth. And would you believe it? It worked! When Hertz had me come to San Francisco to do a travel show, I invited Alice along. The morning after we arrived, I woke up and started to dress. "Where are you going?" asked a groggy Alice. I'd somehow neglected to tell her that I had to perform every day from 10 to 5. She thought we were on vacation. She was not happy. She spent the days at museums, being a tourist. Marc Summers on vacation? Forget it.

On Sundays, we made breakfast together, and then our mission was to clean. We had a stereo, books, the living room, bathroom, kitchen, and bedroom. And we cleaned them all. I dusted all the windowsills. We had venetian blinds, filthy with L.A. smog. There were five windows in the living room and three in the bedroom, all fitted with venetian blinds. Actually, every window in the house had venetian blinds. I'd painstakingly run a rag along each slat, wiping the grime from both sides.

Alice lived up to my standards for bathroom cleaning. She'd scrub and scrub the floor, toilet bowl, bathtub. Lemon pledge wafted through our house. We did the vacuuming. We did the wash. That's the way it was on Sunday. We cleaned all day in our one-bedroom apartment. I didn't like it, but I had to do it. In order to function properly during the week, everything in my brain and in my life had to be in order by Sunday night. I don't know what would have happened if I'd woken up Monday morning and something had been out of place; it never happened.

A few years ago, I asked Alice, "Why did you do it?"

"I thought it was normal, just part of married life," she said.

At the beginning of a relationship you jump through hoops to please your partner. But after a while, you want go to the beach on Sundays, to Fisherman's Village, to walk around and see the shops, to look at the boats.

I wish there had been the knowledge about OCD then that we have today. Alice and I had no idea what was going on; why I exploded, why I was compelled to clean. Today, however, the disorder is identified and out in the open, and there are proven approaches to helping someone you care about who is an obsessive compulsive.

OCD can put a huge strain on relationships. After Alice and I had been married for six years, we felt we were finally ready to start a family. In 1980 Matthew was born, and three years later, Meredith. We were thrilled, but gradually my OCD became torturous for Alice. She felt that my rigid cleanliness and need for order prevented me from living up to my full potential as a loving, embracing father. I was too uptight to have small kids in the house, she said. It took a toll on our marriage. I was frequently consumed with my compulsions when I should have been spending time with my family. I still hadn't heard of OCD then, and unrecognized, untreated OCD is far more devastating for relationships and family life than is managed, acknowledged OCD.

If your date or mate is exhibiting OCD symptoms, the first thing I recommend is not to overreact. Contact a doctor or OCD hotline. Get as much information as possible. Don't say to your partner, "You're crazy." Say, "Can I have a conversation with you? I think there may be something we should look into. Do you think it's normal that you have to flip the light 11 times, check the door 19 times, wash your hands 30 times?" It was at Alice's bidding that I finally sought treatment. And that was the best possible thing for me, for her, and for our kids.

I've met many couples at Foundation meetings, and have seen a wide variety of responses to OCD. I've talked to some couples in which the partner without OCD says, "I will do everything I can to help my mate," and couples in which the non-OCD part-

ner says, "I don't know if I can handle this." I think back to Lorrie and Matt, the lovely couple who appeared with me on the
Oprah show. Matt was an incredibly supportive husband, but a
lack of professional guidance and his love and concern for his
wife led him unwittingly to become an "enabler." Along with Lorrie's mother, Matt helped Lorrie enact her rituals. By helping
Lorrie carry out her compulsions (buying her food five miles
away, bringing her cigarettes in her prescribed manner, assisting
her in her tortured eating rituals) the two people closest to Lorrie
were probably exacerbating her symptoms.

When you are the partner or close loved one of somebody with
OCD, it's important to seek professional help, because strangely
enough, acting on instincts is not always in the best interest of
your loved one. Giving in, reassuring, or debating are generally
not constructive in helping to decrease the symptoms of OCD. It
is an incredibly difficult thing, to refuse to alleviate the fears of
your most dearest, even if you know it's in their best interest. Lorrie's mother said that when she tried not engaging in Lorrie's
mealtime rituals, Lorrie wouldn't eat. There are numerous support groups and family therapy groups which the OC Foundation
or any other of the groups listed at the back of this book can put
you in touch with. You don't have to go it alone.

Once I was diagnosed and began receiving treatment, Alice
and my kids were a great help to me. They still are. My kids say,
"Dad, you're doing that again. You just did that. Do you really
need to neaten your desk again?" I find it very helpful when they
point out my repetitive actions with love and patience. What I
had to do, as the OCD person in the family, was, first, admit that

I had a disorder. The next step was deciding I wanted to get better and stop performing my rituals.

I'm aware of the strain my obsessive compulsive behavior has put on my family, and I'm as understanding as possible. When Alice or someone I really trust tells me, "Hey, you're doing it again," I laugh and say, "You're right!" That helps me say to myself, "Stop it. You don't need to do it."

earthquake

Howard Hughes is the most famous example in our century of someone with OCD. Hughes, who had inherited millions from his father, was a playboy, aviator, inventor, and movie producer. At one time, he was the richest man in America. But throughout his life, Hughes suffered from OCD. He had severe contamination fears. No one could touch his private refrigerator. Like me, he couldn't bear to wear clothing that had the least little spot on it.

Hughes was immensely successful. His OCD probably fostered in him the same kind of drive and perfectionism that has ruled my life. Sadly, his compulsions were doomed to destroy him.

After a near-fatal plane crash, Hughes' OCD intensified. Afraid to go out, to see anyone, or to come in contact with a world he was convinced was full of deadly germs, Hughes lived in self-enforced solitary confinement, holed up in the baronial splendor of his top-floor suite in Acapulco's Princess Hotel. It's hard to visualize how this powerful man went from *bon vivant* to a guy so consumed by his OCD anxieties that he couldn't leave his room.

What's truly striking about Hughes' story is that piloting his airplane, he was totally focused on the task at hand, which was a matter of life and death. I feel that kind of focus every time I'm in front of a camera: my OCD recedes. But there was one short period in my life where I experienced a *complete* remission of my OCD symptoms. It occurred when, like Hughes in his plane, I was completely preoccupied with survival.

It was the winter of 1994. I had finally attained many of the goals I had strived for since I was a kid ogling the credits scrolling at the end of my favorite TV shows. I was in the midst of a long, successful run in my career. In 1986, I had been signed to do *Double Dare.* The show took off: it put Nickelodeon on the map, made me a household name, and had a phenomenally long life, as cable programs go.

Cable television is a unique animal. Sixty-five episodes is the typical limit of almost all cable shows. After that, the show is yanked off the air and sent into reruns. That's how it works. But with *Double Dare* we did 525 episodes between 1986 and 1994, probably more episodes of one show than any cable network has ever done.

In all those years working as the star of what was at that time Nickelodeon's biggest hit, I never knew what was going to happen next season. The Nickelodeon powers that be were always vague. "Do I have a job next year?" I would ask them in so many words. "We don't know," they'd say. That's show business: no matter how high you climb, you're always at someone's beck and call.

By 1994, *Double Dare* had played itself out: Nickelodeon had enough episodes on tape to do reruns forever, so I wasn't surprised when they decided to stop shooting new shows. I then signed a contract with the network to produce and host live performances of *Double Dare*. We took the show on the road, performing on weekends in arenas across the country, often in front of ten or fifteen thousand people.

I'm asked whether I would go back to *Double Dare* if it was resurrected. There are murmurs at Nickelodeon from time to time of doing just that. To slime or not to slime, that is the question. It would be a tough call for me. I want to do adult television; I don't want to be pigeonholed as a kiddy host. But I wouldn't mind going back to *Double Dare* as a producer.

In 1994, I was also working for ABC's *Home Show* as a roving correspondent, which provided me with the opportunity to do serious news. I covered tornadoes in Kansas, the unveiling of the astronaut memorial at Cape Canaveral, and the return of troops from the Gulf War.

The *Home Show* broadcast live at 8:00 A.M. West Coast time, 11:00 A.M. on the East Coast, Monday through Friday. My correspondent job required that I be in the studio only two or three mornings each week. The show shot at ABC studios at Prospect and Talmedge Streets, a seedy part of Hollywood. I had to be there at 5:30 or 6:00 A.M. I'd wake up at four, shower, hop in the car, and get on the Ventura Freeway as dawn washed the sky with beautiful pastel colors in the omnipresent smog. Traffic was light at this time in the morning. But in L.A., people are always on the road, always moving.

The Prospect Street studios had once been used for film, and even though they were old and decaying they had a certain charm. Most television studios in L.A. are enormous cinder block buildings, enclosed universes that look like they could survive a nuclear attack. But at ABC you could wander the lot, from sound stage to sound stage. There was a neat old commissary where, during my warm-up days when *Welcome Back, Kotter* was shot at the studio, I'd see John Travolta lunching with the other sweathogs.

It was a schlep to the studio from our house in West Hills, which is north of Malibu and west of the San Fernando Valley. To make an 8:00 breakfast meeting in Beverly Hills, I'd have to leave the house by 6:00. But the schools were good, and it was an all-around better place to raise a family than anything we could have afforded closer to town.

We had moved to West Hills in 1984, buying a four-bedroom house with a nice backyard. Our neighborhood was exactly like the one in "E.T." Wide, gently winding blacktop sloped up into a middle-class subdivision that had settled into the mountain landscape. The lawns and plantings around each home were irrigated, a lush oasis set in the midst of stark arid hills. The wholesome Main Street, USA innocence of West Hills reminded me of my Midwestern childhood.

One of the perks of broadcasting at 8:00 A.M. was that I was out of the studio by 9:00 or 9:30, and back home by midmorning. I'd hang out with friends, go out to lunch, spend time with Alice. One of the biggest reasons I relished this period was because of the time I was able to spend with my kids.

In the past, I'd had tremendous guilt feelings about leaving my family for work. When Meredith was three and four years old, I was away for months at a time, shooting *Double Dare* in New York and Philadelphia. When I was on the air, she'd search behind the bookcase on which the television sat, saying, "Dada! Dada!" During one period, she was so angry I was away that she refused to speak to me when I called home.

I was there for her third birthday party, though. We had just moved into the house, and my OCD symptoms were strong. The thought of 20 three-year-olds marauding through our pristine space made me anxious enough to try to convince Alice to have the party at a bowling alley, ice cream parlor, McDonald's, anywhere but in our house.

Alice put her foot down: "We bought this house and we're going to use it!" she said.

What to do? The day approached, and I became more and more distraught. Finally, I couldn't bear it: I measured how tall Meredith was, and then I ran out and bought yard upon yard of butcher paper and taped it along the base of the wall to well above the height of your average three-year-old. I taped it to the wooden posts in the corners of the room so the tape wouldn't scuff the paint on the sheetrock.

The neighbors heard about this and came by to see my handiwork, chuckling and shaking their heads.

Our kids grew up in that house. I put up a professional NBA backboard on a pole sunk into the edge of the driveway (if I had put it up over the garage the ball would have made marks on the house), and when I was home Matthew and I played basketball most evenings after dinner. We'd always bonded around sports. We went to batting cages together, and I coached his Little League team. He was fast, a great base-stealer. I loved watching him take off, streaking around the diamond, sliding into second base. He was ballsy, a risk taker, completely unafraid.

Going one-on-one with Matthew on the blacktop in front of the garage, I was my usual competitive self. I never let him win. And not only that, when he was a young kid, I taunted him as I trounced him. The hardest day of my life was the first day he beat me. I had known it was inevitable: he was 12, thin, wiry, already my height, fast as a greyhound and agile. The fateful day came when he was half a step ahead of me, and he beat me by four points. In my mind it might as well have been a thousand.

"A new world champion!" he crowed as the final shot went in, taunting me in the same way I had taunted him. I had to laugh, but I was burning inside. It was payback time, the changing of the guard.

I rarely beat him after that. We'd play as the sun set and the air turned cool: the minty smell of pine and freshly mowed lawns and dry desert night coming down around us. I had mounted lights on the garage, and we'd play into the darkness. The neighborhood kids would be out, rollerblading and riding their bikes and skateboards. They'd often ask to play, and we soon had a game going. When he was young, Matthew and I played against all comers. But after a certain age he wanted to lead his own team to beat me, and I was always ready for the challenge.

On Labor Day, 1993, my life was complete. After much thought, we decided to move into a new house in Mountain View Estates in the city of Calabasas, a five-minute drive from West Hills. The house was 6,000 square feet, a mansion as my friends said, although I didn't think of it that way. Mountain View was a gated community, which I felt we needed at that point in our lives. The popularity of *Double Dare* was such that kids were always showing up at our front door in West Hills. Whenever anyone in the neighborhood had relatives in town, they'd bring them over to meet Marc Summers. Privacy started to become something all of us craved. But then something happened that spurred me to move sooner rather than later. I was working at home in my upstairs office when I suddenly noticed a towheaded kid with pale blue eyes standing on the landing. I was startled. He had come out of nowhere, like an apparition.

"Who are you?" I asked.

"Harold," he said, which struck me as an odd name for one so young.

"What are you doing here?"

"I heard this was where you lived, and I wanted to meet you."

I signed a press photo for him: to Harry from Marc Summers. But he shifted on his feet and looked down at the carpet.

"What's wrong?" I asked.

"Could you make it out to Harold, please?"

I let out a little embarrassed puff of laughter, and he glared at me. I quickly took another press photo from the shelf, inscribed it to his specifications, and then led him downstairs and out the door. I had begun to feel visible and exposed, but this was the capper. Though he was just a kid, having an intruder in my home frightened me. I was traveling a lot, and I wanted the extra protection for Alice, Meredith, and Matthew that a gated community would supply.

The new house was beyond anything I'd ever imagined being able to afford living in. On the wide terrace that connected Meredith's room (French doors, walk-in closet, private bath with Jacuzzi) to the master bedroom, I could look out over the stunning vista from the Santa Monica Mountains to Malibu. I never took the house for granted. I had earned it; nobody gave it to me. But inside, I always felt my family was like the Beverly Hillbillies in this ritzy exclusive community.

That was the way it was the evening of January 13. I went to bed that night next to Alice, happily married, in the house of my dreams with my wonderful family, my career going great guns. As usual I couldn't get to sleep. I always say that if my neighbor sneezes, I wake up. Almost every night I toss and turn, thinking about work, the people I need to call back, the appointments I've scheduled, upcoming travel plans. I find it almost impossible to relax: some nights I don't sleep at all.

It must have been one or two in the morning when I finally drifted off into a dreamless sleep. The next thing I knew I was awake, in the pitch black, feeling intuitively before I could grasp what was going on that something was very wrong. Faintly, on the edge of my hearing, glasses tinkled and there was a tight rumbling. The air was thick and bristling, and then I was wide awake and so was Alice. The house began to shake.

Alice and I had a prearranged earthquake plan. I was responsible for Meredith; she for Matthew. We leapt out of bed. The floor heaved under my feet, the whole house cracking and groaning. I lurched to the door of Meredith's bedroom and then the quake's peak hit. The floor fell away, and I was thrown against the wall. It felt as though a giant had picked up the house and dropped it.

The quake's peak seemed to go on and on, although it probably only lasted a few short seconds. When I finally got to Meredith, she was sitting bolt upright in bed, white as a sheet, in a state of shock. She threw her arms around my neck, and she was trembling and rigid.

Matthew, typically, had slept through the whole thing. He was rubbing his eyes sleepily as we hustled downstairs in our nightclothes. I grabbed the battery-powered radio by our bed and a flashlight. We flung open the front door and ran into the driveway. Car and home alarms were going off, and the whole neighborhood was out on the street in front of their homes. The power was out, and we stood out under the stars, flashlights flickering in the dark.

Living in L.A., it's an accepted fact of life that you don't want to be inside when the big one hits and your house collapses on top of you. It's much better to be tossed around like a piece of popcorn in the open air.

There was an aftershock every couple of minutes, lasting from 5 to 20 seconds. Any one of them could have been bigger than the initial quake. We sat on the stairs by the front door and listened to radio call-ins from reporters and people on the street.

At first, I wasn't thinking about the state of our house. But as dawn broke over the hills, I began to mull over the damage that had been done. When the aftershocks finally quieted, we went back inside, and I toured the house. It had moved, and everything inside it had moved as well. The books, Alice's china cat collection, Meredith's doll collection, everything had all come tumbling off the shelves. There was broken glass everywhere. There were fissures in the walls of every room, and our marble entryway had shifted and cracked.

As I walked through the house, surveying the damage, it began to dawn on me that I didn't feel the need to clean or straighten. I was confronted with the biggest mess of my life, but I didn't care! My OCD seemed to have disappeared, magically vanished. All I was thinking about was my family.

The quake was 6.9 on the Richter scale, and the aftershocks, which came every couple of minutes, were big ones, too: 6.2, 5.9. There was no relief.

Two days after the quake, I did a *Home Show* segment in Northridge, the quake's epicenter. I drove the streets at dawn. It was a weird morning, quiet and still, different from the hum of traffic and movement that always pervades L.A. at any hour of the day or night.

There was destruction everywhere. The streets had buckled and cracked. Streetlights tilted at crazy angles. Trees had toppled onto cars, crushing them. Businesses had plywood covering broken windows. Security guards prowled the streets to keep away looters. It looked like a war zone.

I passed a hospital, where there was a line of people waiting outside for treatment. The night of the quake, fire had erupted in Northridge. A gas main had exploded, and the trees along the street were scorched and charred. I found the house where we were shooting the segment, and we set up to interview its owners, a married couple with kids. They gave me a tour with the camera and audio guys trailing behind us. The house was intact enough to walk through, but barely.

I couldn't believe 22 seconds of the earth's power had destroyed these people's lives. I felt frail, shaky from all that my own family had been through in the last 48 hours. While we were on the air, Gary Collins, who hosted the *Home Show*, asked me, "How are you doing?"

I almost broke down.

Later, I heard that a neighbor of ours had been watching the show while Matthew was visiting her son. The neighbor had snidely said to Matthew that she was surprised at how emotional I had become during the interview. This was Southern California: earthquakes were a part of life.

Her insensitivity infuriated me, but Matthew took her comment with a grain of salt. He's used to having me derided. His friends in school were huge fans of *Double Dare*—until they grew out of it. Then they started making fun of me to his face. I know Matthew: he was loyal. He knew the jabs were part of having a father in the public eye.

Alice's brother, sister-in-law, and mother were worried about structural problems in their apartment building in West L.A., and they moved in with us. Having company, the stress around the earthquake, and, most important, the deplorable state of my house would normally have sent me into an obsessive compulsive frenzy. The desire to order and straighten would have overwhelmed me.

But I was so focused on the welfare of my family that I didn't even notice the chaos that surrounded us. It was an intense relief to be free of the gnawing anxiety to have things perfect.

I've never heard of this kind of spontaneous remission in other OCD sufferers, but it's not uncommon for the reverse to happen: for people to have one bout with OCD in their life and then recover. Someone I'll call Bob, a successful lawyer in the entertainment industry, told me he had severe symptoms of OCD when he was in his stressful first year at Harvard Law School.

When you meet Bob, you'd never think that a man with such poise and confidence, so at ease with people and at home in the world, would have been, at one time, afraid to open the door and walk out of his Cambridge, Massachusetts, apartment. Like Howard Hughes, Bob was convinced he would be contaminated by germs. For several weeks, he cowered in his apartment, consumed by dread. His roommate brought him tins of food, which he ate straight from the can with his hands, which he would meticulously scrub, afraid to let the food touch pots, pans, plates, or even silverware. All of these, he thought, were crawling with deadly germs.

Bob feels that his bout with OCD was brought on by the pressure of final exams. He showed up at the exams with his hands encased in gloves, although the May weather was warm and sunny. After the tests were over (he scored in the top 10 percent of his class), his symptoms vanished, never to return, as mysteriously as they had appeared.

Bob's is not a typical case of OCD, which continues over a long period of time and impacts one's whole life. Many OCD sufferers think that they're going to somehow mysteriously get better. But studies have shown that if you have OCD, you've got it for life.

Howard Stern is an example of someone with OCD who thinks he has somehow mysteriously cured himself of the disorder. He's fooling himself. Howard and I battled it out on the radio one day when I came on his show as the spokesperson for obsessive compulsive disorder. Howard was obviously sympathetic to the OC Foundation cause. He admitted that at one time he had OCD, but he insisted that he had "cured himself."

"You're not cured, Howard," I told him.

He became huffy. "Yes, I am."

"No, you're not!"

He said he had cured himself of his OCD in the same way he had cured himself of back pain: he realized that it was psychosomatic and had no basis in physical reality. He told his listeners about his bizarre rituals: banging his head 16 times before going on the air to make sure the show went well; mentioning a certain number in every sentence to ward off disaster when he was on the air; believing that even numbers were good and odd numbers were bad (then, somehow, they switched); being a germphobic and an obsessive hand washer to the point where he had his own bathroom built in the radio studio.

"Howard," I said. "You acted that way because your brain chemistry is screwed up."

"No way!" he said. "Absolutely not!"

Robin Quivers, his longtime foil, started goading him.

"Howard," she said. "Aren't you a hypochondriac?"

At the time of my appearance on the show, Stern had lightly bruised his ankle. He had just recently been obsessing on the small injury, overwhelmed by intrusive thoughts, convinced that the bruise would lead to a debilitating condition that would fell him.

Robin kept badgering him. "It's ridiculous, Howard, admit it!" Finally he acquiesced.

"Okay, okay, okay!" he said. "But that's not OCD. I'm cured."

I laughed as he quickly went to take calls from listeners.

After the show, I told Howard that OCD is not like depression. With depression, you can suddenly become better without going through treatment. But he fixated on the idea that he no longer suffered from the disorder. After appearing with him, I thought about my own spontaneous cure, and how short-lived it was.

After the earthquake, I wanted to talk to my shrink about the sudden relief from my cleaning compulsions, intrusive thoughts, and ridiculous rituals. I didn't know I had OCD, but I did know I had been carrying around a deep dark secret, thinking I was crazy for as long as I could remember. Now that I was symptom-free, I was finally ready to confess to someone just how weird I had been.

I had started therapy in the early 1980s with a psychiatrist who I'll call William. I was frustrated with busting my butt but not getting anywhere in my career. I saw everyone else in my clique at the Comedy Store (David Letterman, Jay Leno, Robin Williams, and Garry Shandling) becoming famous. But I seemed stuck in the land of perpetual warm-ups. I was making good money, but I was bored. That changed after I scored on *Double Dare*, but I kept going to William, occasionally seeing him when I felt overwhelmed by life. I'd go to him for two or three sessions and then wouldn't call him again for six months.

I told him intimate parts of my life, but I had never touched on my OCD symptoms. I thought I was the only person in the world with my symptoms. I was profoundly afraid to talk about them, so afraid that not even Alice knew about my intrusive thoughts and secret rituals.

William's office had been trashed by the earthquake, so he had moved to the Agoura area. His new space was off the Ventura Freeway, in one of southern California's ubiquitous strip malls.

A tall man in his late forties with prematurely gray hair and a soft, soothing voice, William rose to greet me as I entered the office. You had to listen closely to catch his words. He was always calm and collected, and he was very successful. We had a little ritual at the beginning of each session.

"So, Marc," William began, "tell me about your dreams."

"I don't dream."

"Yes, you do."

That's how it went.

During this session, for the first time, I told William about my compulsions to clean and straighten: I had to vacuum in perfect rows, no one could touch the walls in our home, as a child I had secret rituals that I performed so my parents wouldn't die. And, in fact, I still had such rituals: if I didn't correctly read my script for the show, disaster would befall me or my loved ones.

He listened with his mouth hanging open. "Very interesting," he said, when I was finally finished.

"But Doc, now I don't feel compelled to do that stuff. I think I'm cured."

We spent the whole hour talking about my "odd behaviors," and how none of them meant anything anymore.

Had William recognized my odd behaviors as classic symptoms of OCD, he might have been able to resolve my problem. I still wonder what my life would have been like if he had caught the disorder years before it was eventually diagnosed by Dr. Hollander. As it turned out, William was clueless about OCD. But he was very excited about the earthquake session. We decided the quake had been a terrific thing for me.

"Do you mind if I mention your case in an article?" he asked. He wanted to write up how his patient had been cured by the great earthquake. I went to see him two or three weeks in a row, continuing to talk about the absence of my drives to straighten.

Years later, after my diagnosis, I called William. I told him that the whole time I was his patient I was suffering from OCD.

"You never suspected it?" I asked him, incredulous.

"Nope." He was not the least bit apologetic. "The thought never crossed my mind."

Whenever I talk about OCD, people suffering from the disorder tell me horror stories about misdiagnosis. I've heard countless times that someone spent years and thousands of dollars in therapy only to be told that his fanatical need to clean or wash his hands came from his potty training when he was two years old. A few years ago, I was at an American Psychiatric Association Convention, signing a book by Connie Foster about children with OCD for which I had written the foreword. A psychiatrist walked by and asked me what I was doing.

"We're trying to help out kids with OCD," I told him.

"Oh," he snorted, "I never see anyone like that!" I stared after him, incredulous. Two to three percent of the population has OCD, and many find their way to a psychiatrist's office, only to face a doctor with almost no knowledge of the disorder. Of course he had patients with OCD. He just hadn't diagnosed them correctly.

Unfortunately, my remission was too good to last. My obsessive compulsive behavior came roaring back, sparked by a particularly severe aftershock that occurred exactly one month after the big quake. That one month was the only time since I was about six or seven years old that I wasn't plagued by compulsions.

Alice and I were driving in West L.A. when the aftershock sent our car lurching across the road. I took Alice to her mom's and rushed home. The mirrors and paintings were askew. There were a few odds and ends lying on the floor, and I was surprised that I didn't rush to clean them up immediately. I felt remarkably calm given the circumstances.

Then I went into the family room. A big wooden bowl had fallen off the top of a shelf, gouging a big chink in our beautiful oak floor. I stood there looking at this hideous blight, feeling the anxiety well up inside me. It was a defamation, a desecration. I wanted to scream. I crashed straight from sanity into the sense that my life wasn't perfect—and that I *needed* it to be perfect or I'd go nuts. In our old house, I'd lived through the mess of having the floors stripped, sanded, and stained. Now we would have to live with that misery again because there was a chip in the floor. There was *absolutely no way* it could stay. As I stared at the chink in the floor, the infinite things pushed out of place in the house by the quake descended upon me like the plagues on Pharaoh.

The aftershocks went on for months, during which time I had

to live with the cracks in the walls and floor. It was useless to try to fix them before the earth settled. I tried to cope by spending lots of time out of the house. And when the aftershocks finally abated and the renovations began, I tried not to go into the rooms under repair. The upstairs was in better shape than the ground floor, so that's where I spent most of my time when I was home.

When I did have to go downstairs, I'd stand on the top floor landing, knowing that downstairs I would see the corners and joints in the living room where the walls had separated. I'd find myself returning to the same crack in the wall over and over again, staring transfixed in front of it as though it was a mesmerizing work of art. Had it widened slightly? Or was it mysteriously coming back together?

Forcing myself to walk away, I'd be drawn irresistibly back against my will. It was a morbid fascination. It was grotesque, yet somehow it transfixed me. I stared and stared. I went away. And then I came back to stare some more.

the moment of truth

I'd always wanted to host my own live talk show. *Marc Summers, Live from New York City!* I'd hosted game shows: *Double Dare, Family Double Dare, What Would You Do, Couch Potatoes,* and *Pick Your Brain.* I had also produced *Double Dare* and created, hosted, and produced *Pick Your Brain.* They had been "mine." But to do a live talk show? I loved the prospect of working live, of talking to a potpourri of guests: celebrities, authors, quirky people. For me, a live talk show was the best of television. From 1990 to 1994, I had been a contributing reporter on ABC's *Home Show.*

I was disappointed when *The Home Show* was canceled, but word was out that Lifetime Television was creating a new show and looking to me to handle it. I walked from one job to another.

The smooth transition was fortunate: I'd noticed when there was stress in my work life, I'd start cleaning fanatically. I couldn't bear to have the house messy. I couldn't even bear the thought that the house might *become* messy. I couldn't tolerate it when my son or daughter wanted to have friends over who might make a mess, scuff up the carpets, leave crumbs on the floors, or inadvertently move the furniture. I needed the whole house to have the feel of a museum: immaculate and untouched.

Under stress, I'd begin to have anxious thoughts. Not the kind of morbid thoughts that I'd had as a child, when I thought my parents would die if I didn't read a paragraph "perfectly." But anxious feelings that led to repetitious rituals: the compulsion to make lists and go over and over them in my mind, as I had as a child; a fanatical need to arrange knickknacks; hours spent on my hands and knees on our wooden floors, rubbing out the slightest scuff-marks.

I was offered the job hosting the Lifetime show *Our Home,* which was designed to scoop up the *Home Show* viewers. The show shot in New York City, to which I moved in 1994. I took a ridiculously expensive apartment on 56th Street and Second Avenue and commuted back and forth to L.A. to see my family, whom I missed terribly. But *Our Home* was not only a great career opportunity, it was extremely high-paying. At this point in my career, I was one of the highest-paid people on cable.

I was the only man on Lifetime Television, which billed itself as television for women. "Great job you've got," people used to tell me. "Being the only guy in a sea of women."

Our Home gave instruction in everything from faux marble painting to new cooking techniques from some of the world's best chefs, who came on the show direct from New York City's finest restaurants. Initially we shot the show at 57th Street and 10th Avenue, and eventually moved to a studio in Astoria, Queens. Several months into the program, I guested on *Queens*, a Lifetime talk show hosted by Sissy Biggers and shot in a basement studio in that same building in Astoria. Sissy and I hit it off immediately.

We were total opposites. I was a Jewish guy from a middle-class family in the Midwest. Sissy was a tony East Coast blueblood, 5' 2", slender, stylish, with short blond hair. She knew all the hip fashions and loved to hang with an old-school moneyed crowd. She was extremely well connected because of the years she had spent as an executive at NBC, where she had handled *The David Letterman Show* and *Saturday Night Live*. It was an unusual transition, going from executive to working on-camera, but she'd always wanted to be a TV personality.

Sissy loved to go out in the evening, romping around the city with celebrities while I holed up in my apartment, read the script for the next day's show, talked to my family on the phone, and watched TV. I teased her about her social activities, and spun ridiculous tales of eating at fancy restaurants and hobnobbing with stars.

Upper management at Lifetime had me guest on Sissy's show a couple more times, to be sure the initial chemistry wasn't a fluke. They loved us together; we were incredibly compatible.

Sissy was very sensitive to how I was feeling, what was going on in my mind. Management was so impressed with our rapport that they decided to create a show specially for us. They found a new host for *Our Home*, and *Biggers and Summers* was born.

I had a show. A live talk show! Monday through Friday, 11 A.M. to noon. I was thrilled. It was exactly where I wanted to be. (Well, I would have preferred to be on a network, of course, and then in syndication. But I figured they'd try to syndicate the show: we had a clause in our contract explicitly stating the terms should the show be syndicated.)

We covered topics from celebrities and health to lifestyle and fashion. Our guests all had something to push, plug, or sell—we gave them a platform and they gave us something to talk about every morning. We were hip. We were fun. We were *Biggers and Summers.*

Shooting out in Astoria was a drag. I had come to New York to do a show in Manhattan, not to cross the 59th Street Bridge into the boroughs. But Astoria did have some perks. Don Imus, Sesame Street, and Bill Cosby had their shows there. It was where Bette Midler, Diane Keaton, and Goldie Hawn had shot *The First Wives Club.* To my daughter's great delight, I once rode the elevator with Leonardo DiCaprio. The studio was an exciting place to work: there was always a celebrity in the elevator or down the hall.

I found the one hour a day doing live television to be an enormous emotional relief. Whenever I was on the air, the stresses, strains, and loneliness of the life I had in New York, far from my wife and children, evaporated. When the cameras rolled, I was on another planet—planet TV—where I felt completely comfortable, totally in control. When I was off-camera I felt isolated and off balance, prey to constant low-grade obsessive compulsive anxieties that would flare up at odd moments.

I was living in a spacious rental apartment, which I kept neat as a pin. First thing every morning, I made the bed. The spread didn't have a wrinkle on it. It looked like a sheet of ice. Before going to sleep each night, I spent 10 minutes fluffing and arranging the pillows on the couch. Even with all these details taken care of, during the evenings I would always have a lot of trouble concentrating: when I went over the script for the following day's show, I'd read the same paragraph again and again without absorbing it.

In New York, the most disturbing symptom of my disorder occurred not in my apartment but on Madison Avenue. I'd walk up and down Madison when I returned to Manhattan after a day in the Queens studio. I would read the signs in the shop windows over and over again. If I didn't read the signs correctly, I was convinced Meredith wouldn't get a part in the school play or Matthew wouldn't make the sports team. I was afraid that if I didn't read the sign just right, the plane I took every Thursday to California would crash.

I obsessed endlessly about those Thursday flights, following strict rituals to ensure that disaster didn't strike. I was especially drawn to the window of one particular watch store. I vividly remember standing in front of the store's window one blustery fall evening. A sale was on for Breitling watches. There was a sign in the window that explained the watches' special features: dual time zones, perpetual calendar, day-and-date display. I read the sales pitch from top to bottom at least 25 times, a sickening feeling gripping my stomach and chest, utterly convinced that if I

didn't read the ad copy perfectly my plane would hurtle down-
ward in a ball of flame somewhere over Missouri.

Reading perfectly meant with complete fluidity, without hesi-
tation, from beginning to end. Even the slightest moment of dis-
traction, the least little glitch in the smoothness of the way the
words scrolled in my mind, and I would be compelled to start
over from the beginning. I must have read that sign over and over
for nearly half an hour before I finally got it right.

My weekly commute to and from L.A. was a nightmare.
Matthew was 13 and Meredith 10. I'd get into L.A. at 5:00 or 6:00
P.M. on Thursday, and leave for New York again on Sunday. Soon,
I started leaving later and later on Sundays, in order to spend
precious extra hours with my family. Eventually, I was leaving
L.A. at 4:00 P.M. Sunday and getting back to New York at mid-
night. It was difficult for all of us.

For two years this misery continued. Sometimes Matthew and
Meredith wanted to do things with their friends on weekends, but
they felt obligated to stay home and spend time with me, since I
was away all week. My kids didn't want to move East: they were
in the middle of their lives. Alice's mother wasn't well, and Alice
wanted to be with her on the West Coast. So I made the regular
3,000-mile weekend commute.

My phone bills were enormous. I talked to Alice seven times
a day; called the kids two or three times each night. Meredith and
I did her homework on the phone. On the upside (and I always
like to look on the upside), the kids spent summers with me.
They both liked to visit the East Coast, and I was off the air at
noon, so we'd have the whole afternoon to play.

We loved walking around the city. I remember riding the elevator in my apartment building with Meredith one summer when she was staying with me.

"Dad," she said, "I want hot dogs for dinner, and I want to cook at home."

I gulped. The lady across from us in the elevator watched intently. She was older, conservative, with a snooty, uppity upper East Side attitude. I thought hard for a long moment, trying to figure out how to phrase what I wanted to say. "Meredith, my goal is to never use that kitchen."

The lady in the elevator raised her eyebrows.

I wanted to keep the kitchen perfect. The apartment had been completely redone before I moved in, and I was not going to be the first person to despoil its pristine surfaces. I also knew that a hot dog dinner was going to cost me $100, because I had no pots or pans. I couldn't just go out and buy a $5 pot—that's not the way I do things. If I bought anything, it would have to be an entire set of matching pots and pans. But Meredith wanted hot dogs. And macaroni and cheese. So we walked to Macy's, bought pots and pans, and had our dinner. It was warm and close.

We cleaned up. But after Meredith was asleep, I went back into the kitchen and recleaned it, buffing the countertops and the stovetop with paper towels until they gleamed. When I was done in the wee hours of the morning, only the most discerning eye (mine) could tell that the kitchen had ever been used.

I was 43 years old. I had been driven by these compulsions for as long as I could remember. I thought I was just someone who liked a neat, clean house. A man who liked everything in its place. I had no idea there was something wrong with me. But that was about to change.

It was a warm summer evening. Meredith and I had just finished a meal of Chinese take-out. The lights in the buildings of
midtown were coming on, glimmering in the dusk. Traffic flowed
south down Second Avenue, a river of light and movement. The
sounds of the city were faint through the thick glass of the living-
room window and the soothing hiss of central air-conditioning.
I felt good. The show that day had gone well, and I was about
to prepare for the following day's show. Meredith was watching
television.

Prepping for my role as talk show host was nothing like my
tortured attempts to do homework in high school. The producers
lined up our topics and guests and did the research necessary to
keep Sissy and me from looking foolish, assuming we reviewed
the material they prepared for us. I'd usually spend an hour going through the material, a little longer if the following day's
guest was an author. I'd focus on two or three passages of his or
her book, so I'd be able to engage in an informed discussion.

Tomorrow's guests were Dr. Eric Hollander, a New York psychiatrist and director of the "Compulsive, Impulsive, and Anxiety Disorders Program" at Mt. Sinai Hospital, and Mariette
Hartley, a well-known actress and television host, who had written *Breaking the Silence*, a book about alcoholism in her family.

Mariette wasn't coming on the show to discuss her career or
her alcoholic father, but to talk about her role as the National
Spokesperson for the Obsessive Compulsive Foundation. My
producers had provided information from the Foundation on
OCD and its symptoms.

"Some symptoms," I read, "are neatness, checking, cleaning,

placing things symmetrically, compulsive rereading, retracing, intrusive thoughts."

I recognized myself instantly. I couldn't read anymore. I was choked up. My heart was racing. I threw the papers down, stood up, and paced around the room. What I had just read described my habits perfectly. It made me nuts; I was freaked out. I needed time to absorb the information, but my immediate concern was the show the following day. Should I let Sissy handle it? If I talked about OCD, would I be able to get through the segment without breaking down? Could I, should I, go on the air and pretend that I didn't think I had the illness?

True to form, I was more worried about my job performance than anything else. Meredith was in the next room, oblivious to my inner turmoil. I didn't want to alarm her. When she came in to say goodnight, I acted as if nothing was wrong.

Before that evening, I had never heard of obsessive compulsive disorder, even though I'd been working in the media for years. I was stunned: it was clear to me I'd been afflicted with the disorder since I had been a child, and, not once, even with all my blatant mannerisms and public rituals, had anyone suggested that I might have OCD.

That was five years ago. Today, far more people are aware of OCD. But there are still many people who have never heard of the disorder. Each time I discuss OCD in public I get letters that read, "Thank God this thing has a name. I really thought I was crazy. Thank you."

Relief is the typical reaction of people who suddenly find out that they're not crazy but are instead victims of treatable disease.

It's still a shock to realize that your brain chemistry differs from most of the rest of humanity's.

I didn't sleep at all that night. I kept thinking: do I avoid the fact that I have the disorder? Do I try and fake it? What was best for me as a performer? What was best for the program? I had never dissembled on the air. I had always tried to play the what-you-see-is-what-you-get type of host.

I reviewed my life. The Sunday cleaning binges. Pacing around the living room with my mother, waiting for my father to come home. Reading and rereading the signs on Madison Avenue. I realized that one of the reasons I had been keeping the apartment neat was that I was afraid if I didn't I would flub my performance on *Biggers and Summers*. The material I read said OCD could be genetically inherited, and I began to suspect that both my parents were afflicted with the disorder.

It was a lot to absorb, and I tossed and turned. But when I climbed out of bed the following morning, I wasn't tired in the least. I woke Meredith up, since she was coming to the studio with me that morning. We had a quick breakfast and then a car service picked us up to take us to the studio. It was one of those hideous New York August mornings. Although it was still early, the pavement was hot and steamy as we left the sanctum of the air-conditioned lobby of my apartment building and ducked into the backseat of the black Lincoln that sat idling at the curb.

I was nervous on the way to Astoria and barely said a word to Meredith. She looked out the window at the sparkling surface of the East River, the tram swinging on its high wire, making its way toward Roosevelt Island. The sun blazed through a heavy haze of humidity and exhaust. We glided along in the air-conditioned car, sunk in its plush upholstery. My palms were sweating, while my fingers were ice-cold.

At the studio, Meredith went to hang out in the makeup room while I met with Sissy and the show's producers in the Green Room. We sat in the same spot every morning—Sissy and I on the big black couch, the producers around the coffee table.

The meeting's first few minutes were light and breezy. We chatted about who had appeared the night before on *Politically Incorrect, The Tonight Show,* and *David Letterman,* until, in the midst of the typical chaos that goes on before live television (late guests, lost guests, technical problems), we focused for 45 minutes, talking down the show (an industry phrase that means going through the show segment by segment). The producer who put together each segment told us what the guests wanted to discuss, what they didn't want to discuss, what they were plugging, critical questions to ask, and what to get to if we had time.

I couldn't concentrate. I got emotional. Finally, I just got it over with. I told them all I thought I had OCD. "I don't know if I can go on," I said. "I might have to walk out during the taping."

I put my head in my hands. Tears squeezed from the corners of my eyes. Everyone was supportive, though. Sissy said, "You open it up, Marc. See how you feel. If you can't continue, just leave. We'll handle it."

As soon as Dr. Hollander arrived at the set, I approached him and introduced myself.

"I think I have OCD," I said.

Dr. Hollander is tall and donnish. He looks far too young to be as smart and knowledgeable as he is. "Why do you think so?" he asked.

I described my symptoms. I might, indeed, have obsessive compulsive disorder, he told me. But he cautioned me that lots of people have traces of OCD, and that I shouldn't jump to conclusions. He gave me his card and told me we could talk after the show.

Air time, 11:00, arrived as it always did. I felt raw. TV had never made me nervous, but that day I was queasy. Sissy and I chatted as usual on a predetermined topic: her life in Connecticut, her kids, her husband's road trip, my family, the fantastic things I'd done the evening before in Manhattan. (I always made my social life seem much grander than it actually was in order to have comic biplay with Sissy.) I was stiff. I was talking—my mouth was moving and sounds were coming out—but I was in a fog, the whole time thinking about the upcoming topic.

We went to commercial break and returned with Dr. Hollander and Mariette Hartley. Dr. Hollander began defining OCD. As he described intrusive thoughts, the compulsion for rituals, and fanatical neatness, the pressure built inside me. I couldn't meet his eyes. I felt numb. Suddenly, I leaned forward.

"Dr. Hollander, I think I have this," I said.

I confessed that I was the father of the only five-year-old in the world who could eat a chocolate ice cream cone without spilling a drop on himself. And I'd been proud of it! For years, I had been forcing my compulsions on my kids. I told a story about getting a call from Matthew's nursery school teacher. In all her years of teaching, our son was the first kid who refused to finger paint because he didn't want to get his hands dirty. Matthew's teacher had asked me to go buy finger paints and show Matthew that getting green gobs of goo under his fingernails was okay. I completed my assignment, despite my total aversion to having paint under my nails. The following Monday at school, Matthew proudly completed his first finger painting.

When we went to a commercial break, I took the deepest breath of my life. Dr. Hollander, who was very approachable, told me, in his soothing bedside manner, "You may find that you do better with treatment. Help is available when you want it."

Later, Dr. Hollander would tell me that I seemed anxious and agitated when I spoke to him before the show.

"You were pacing back and forth, Marc," he said. "You had a pained look on your face. I was surprised when you brought up your OCD on the show. I thought it was a brave, courageous thing you did."

Everyone in the studio wanted to make sure I was okay, and told me I'd done a terrific job. Exercise guru and flamboyant personality Richard Simmons, who'd been another guest that morning, hugged me. "That was a very brave, good thing you just did," he told me. "You helped a lot of people." I welcomed the support, considering the doubt coursing through me—had it been a bad move to "out" myself on the air? How would the viewers react? Would it hurt my career? What would my family think? What now?

I called my parents afterward to discuss the show. I knew they'd seen it. They watched every single one of my shows (you know Jewish parents). They were nervous.

"Do you think that was a smart thing you did?" my mother asked. "Don't you think it will hurt your career?"

My father said he felt the same way.

Later my parents would express their personal discomfort and fear at the public disclosure of my OCD.

After an article appeared in *People* magazine about me coping with the disorder, my dad said, "Just because you're in the public eye doesn't mean we have to be in it, too." My parents felt exposed in their tight-knit Indianapolis community. They thought having a son with OCD was a put-down in their friends' eyes. I tried to reassure them that my OCD had nothing to do with them. It was something I was born with: it wasn't their fault.

I phoned Alice to tell her about the show. She, too, was concerned that I had damaged my career, but on the whole, she was extremely supportive. She said I sounded happy and excited; she was glad I had finally found an answer, a name to put to the behaviors that had perplexed us since our explosive wedding day.

"Things fit together for me," Alice said in a television interview, remembering that call. "Marc's OCD had put a strain on our marriage. I wouldn't say it was a major strain. We tried to make a joke of it. Before Marc talked to Dr. Hollander he and I had chalked his odd behavior up to 'eccentricity.' It was perplexing. His inflexible neatness put a strain on our kids, and I was in the middle. That was difficult for me. I was happy when we got an answer. And I knew Marc. He's an extremely capable man. He *always* follows through. I knew whatever lay ahead, he would overcome it and we would come through it stronger."

It moved me that Alice had such faith in me. And, finally, for the first time in our relationship, I could admit to her (and to myself) how deeply my rituals and anxieties disturbed me. I could finally share that part of myself with her, which was an enormous relief and brought us even closer together.

Before Dr. Hollander left the Astoria studios, he gave me his card. I tucked it into my pocket. But I knew I wouldn't call him. "I can handle this on my own," I thought. "Now I know that what I've been doing all these years has a name, and so I'm fine."

The reaction I had turns out to be a common one among people who have OCD. On average, it takes us seven years from the onset of symptoms to the admission that obsessive compulsive thoughts and behaviors are caused by the disorder. And once we discover we have OCD, we don't seek help for another ten years. We fool ourselves into thinking we're in control.

While I insisted to myself that I was doing fine, secretly one of the reasons I knew I wouldn't call Hollander was because I was scared: I couldn't stand the idea of taking pills. On the show, Hollander had talked about medication as key to treating the disease. I hate to take even an aspirin, so it was horrifying to contemplate taking pills every day to get better. Aversion to pills is common among OCD sufferers and contributes to the delay between diagnosis and treatment.

But something else even more profound keeps many people with OCD from seeking treatment: the stigma surrounding mental illness. Countless obsessive compulsives say that fear of ridicule was what kept them from seeking help or even admitting to themselves that they had the disorder.

I'm encouraged by the recent attention the media has given OCD. Daytime talk shows have been instrumental in spreading the message that different doesn't equal bad, and illness or disability doesn't mean crazy or worthless. Jack Nicholson's Academy Award-winning portrayal of a severe OCD sufferer in *As Good As It Gets* did incalculable good. With every *Oprah, Date-*

line, 20/20, or *Biggers and Summers* show on OCD, someone out there suffering from the disorder feels less alone. With each *People* magazine or *USA Today* article that gives us glimpses of the "normal," healthy, productive people who happen to have OCD, someone suffering in silence is encouraged to take that next step toward getting help.

Along with the media attention, organizations such as the OC Foundation and many other groups listed in the resource guide at the back of this book have turned around the lives of countless sufferers of the disorder.

The week I identified my disorder on the air, thousands of calls flooded the Obsessive Compulsive Foundation's 1-800 number. The PR firm handling the Foundation called me to say it had been a terrific segment; the public's reaction had been tremendous. They asked if I'd be interested in working alongside Mariette, or even in her place. No way, I said. Not a chance. I didn't want to be identified as the guy with OCD.

A couple weeks later the PR firm called and asked again. This time I told them to let me think about it. I called publicists and agents to ask their advice. How would I be viewed? Public service jobs are viewed differently in the industry than they are by the general public. People in the industry tend to think that if someone is crusading for a cause it means they've got nothing else going on work-wise. It is viewed as a move someone makes when his or her career is waning.

The agents I talked to reassured me. They said that so many famous people are confessed drug addicts and alcoholics, becoming known as "the guy with OCD" was a gift in comparison. I finally decided that working on behalf of OCD awareness was the right thing to do. I remembered my early dream to be a rabbi, and I thought: here is my chance to do good, to help people, to make a difference.

But I still didn't call Dr. Hollander. I didn't think of needing help myself, or of the way I tortured myself and occasionally those nearest and dearest to me. I thought, instead, of helping all the OCD sufferers sitting by their phones, staring at the Foundation's number or the number of their doctor. People who desperately needed help but were afraid to call. People who were practicing their inflexible rituals, who were consumed by anxiety but, for whatever reason, were in denial. I still separated myself from those tortured souls. I could not yet admit that I, too, was ill. I was one of them.

rock bottom

"Oh! Blessed rage for order, pale Ramon . . ."
—Wallace Stevens,
The Idea of Order at Key West

In February of 1996, six months after Dr. Hollander appeared on *Biggers and Summers*, the show was canceled. Sissy and I stepped offstage after a Thursday filming and the programming people came over and said, "You just did your last show." That's how it is in TV. They don't want you to bad-mouth the station or the program on the air, so they give no warning when they cancel you. We were lucky. Generally, when a show is canceled they escort the staff directly from the building. The *Biggers and Summers* people were nice; they gave us a week to get out.

Lifetime paid out our contract, which ran for another five

months. "Why can't we stay, then?" I asked the head of programming. "It doesn't make sense to pay us and not use us."

My plea fell on deaf ears. We were done taping new shows as of that day and paid an arm and a leg not to work.

I was never given a clear answer about why we were canceled. Was it because Sissy and I pressed for more publicity for the show or complained about taping in Astoria rather than in Manhattan? The network might have thought we were too uppity. We were supposed to take whatever Lifetime dished out and be grateful. Were we canceled as punishment for bad behavior? For making waves?

Sissy and I were told our show "just wasn't working." Our ratings were middling, as were our ad revenues. We hadn't set the world on fire. But that's the way it is in daytime television on cable—every show gets about the same rating. I felt that management's expectations were unreasonable, especially given the fact that they had done nothing to promote the show.

Although there was some acrimony at the time, Lifetime and I didn't part on bad terms. The old saying "You'll never work in this town again until I need you!" held true for me. You don't want to burn your bridges in television, and so you want to make sure you're nice to everyone. Doug Herzog, the guy who held my cue cards on CNN's *Lee Leonard Show*, now heads Fox Television. It's the same pool of people holding different and better jobs. It just doesn't pay to make enemies.

Sissy took our cancellation harder than I did. She hadn't come to realize the sad truth of television: eventually you're going to get canceled or canned. It's only a matter of time. She eventually ended up on the TV Food Network hosting a game show called

Ready, Set, Cook, which is what she does today. Sissy and I are both driven to be on camera. That's essential for a television personality; you have to want to be there. If you don't, the audience will sense it.

Since I was back living full-time in our L.A. home, I had to break the lease on my New York City apartment with seven months left. At $3,200 a month, that wasn't a small chunk of change for an unemployed guy. But in a bizarre twist of fate, the kind that sometimes seems to come around just when you need it, my daughter's soccer coach's wife's brother was my landlord, who, courtesy of that great connection, was willing to negotiate: if I got out in 12 days he wouldn't hold me to my lease.

Alice flew to New York to help pack up the apartment. We kicked around the city between bouts of packing and labeling boxes. I had developed a love-hate relationship with New York. I loved the pace, the action, the ambition, the professionalism of the city. But I regularly got into or witnessed at least one fight a day living there, with dry cleaners, cab drivers, shopkeepers, anyone and everyone. I got into a fight with the dry cleaner because my shirts came back with black spots. The cleaners insisted the spots were on the shirts when I brought them in. One night my cab slammed into another cab. Both drivers jumped out. My guy was a wiry Asian who started yelling at the other driver, a heavy-set black guy. The other guy punched my guy in the face and knocked him out flat on his back in the middle of Sixth Avenue. Another time, I hailed a cab in the rain, and as I was getting into it, an older woman came up and started beating me on the shins with her umbrella. "That's my cab, Sonny," she said, and pushed me aside and jumped in.

At first it had been fun, but all the attitude and the constant confrontations had begun to wear on me. I was washed out, on edge. I just wanted to relax and be in a place where people were friendly and polite. I won't say L.A. is a bastion of civility (it's not nearly as calm as Indianapolis, for example), but it's more laid-back than New York, sunnier in both weather and temperament.

After Alice returned to L.A., I spent a few days in the city on my own. I wandered the streets, thinking about the ups and downs of the volatile life I had chosen for myself. It was a cold, bleak time. The city seemed strange. I didn't feel part of its life and vitality anymore. I was a ghost wandering through the dark streets and freezing pavement, coming home to an empty apartment that felt like a waiting room for transit to God-knows-where. On Madison Avenue I practiced my sign-reading rituals, only instead of Matthew's success in basketball tryouts, I fixated on what I saw as my future job possibilities. I hadn't the slightest idea of what awaited me in L.A.

Finally, the day came to leave the city. I closed the door on my apartment for the last time and heard the familiar faint sound of wind, a subdued whoosh from the heating vents in the hall. I stood in the elevator with its banks of glowing numerals, my luggage at my feet. It was cold on the street, with stark February early-morning light. I waited under the long canopy of the awning outside while the doorman flagged me a cab. He put my bags in the trunk and I bid him farewell and tipped him. I slid into the cab's backseat, leaning back as we accelerated off the curb into the jockeying traffic, bouncing over manhole covers, idling at cross-street lights, and then taking the hard turn onto the FDR Drive, the first leg of the short journey to Kennedy Airport.

On the plane, I looked out the portal into a vista of cloudless blue sky. I thought about my dreams to host a television show in New York City, and how that dream had come briefly to life and then faded, as dreams always do, in the harsh light of day.

Alice picked me up at LAX. We drove north along the freeways, through the dazzling midday sun, up the coast to our new home north of Malibu in the plush bedroom community of Calabasas. We'd bought a new house during the period when I was commuting between New York and L.A., and I didn't feel entirely at home in it yet. If Alice was cooking and asked me to pass her a ladle, I didn't know where to start looking for it—extremely disconcerting for a guy who has to have everything just so.

I had been making a small fortune for the past couple of years, but our cash flow would soon dwindle to nothing if I didn't get more work. Alice and I had been poor when we were young. But it's different to face hard financial times in middle age. There was the kids' college tuition to think about, and our future retirement. Plus, we had grown accustomed to a high standard of living that would be hard to relinquish.

I keenly felt my responsibility as a father and husband. I looked back at my career path, and I wondered how I had come to this point in my life. I was feeling my age in a town and a business that can make you feel over the hill at 40. I looked back at my life and tallied my accomplishments. It seemed that everything I had worked for had come to nothing. I was faced with the prospect of living off dribs and drabs of ever-shrinking residuals and royalties.

I obsessed, going over and over my career path, trying to identify the misstep that had led to my present sorry state. I obsessed over money. When I first started doing warm-ups for sitcoms and game shows in 1974, I was paid $160 a night. By 1982, warm-ups were still my primary source of income, but I was making $1,200 a night.

After 1982 I moved from doing warm-ups to hosting rehearsals for game shows. The rehearsals were dry runs of the shows that were done before a live audience but weren't taped. Rehearsals paid better than the warm-ups, but they still were nowhere near as well paid as hosting the shows themselves. The game shows in those days were an old boys' club. The hosts were older men with gray hair. They jealously guarded the gates of a closed world, partially because the money was so good: they made $10,000 and up per week, and they didn't want to share the spoils with any young upstarts.

There was an irony in this because the game shows had a tainted feel. They were looked at as the bargain basement of daytime television, which was looked at as the bargain basement of television by the show business world. Daytime personalities are perceived in New York and L.A. as people who can't make it at night. But that's not true. Look at Rosie or Oprah. They work brilliantly on daytime, but I don't think they'd work nearly as well at night.

Back in L.A. I keenly felt the stigma attached to game shows. I had experienced the higher reaches of daytime television with *Biggers and Summers* and in my work as a roving correspondent for the *Home Show*. The *Home Show* was network. If you work on a major network, you've arrived. Both the *Home Show* and *Biggers and Summers* were informational live television, with that sense of excitement of working without the safety net of editing.

The prospect of going back to being dipped in goo or taking part in the shenanigans of game shows felt like a huge step backward.

Not that I was being offered a game show. This was the first time I'd been unemployed since 1978, and I'd been working seven days a week since 1986. There was a time when I had four shows on the air simultaneously, hosting all of them and producing some. My work provided income, which was, of course, extremely important, but it was also a way for me to channel an aspect of my disease: my need to win, to be perfect, to be the best; to accumulate as many credits as possible and reach the pinnacle of my career. People would tell me, "I can't turn on the TV without seeing you." "Good!" I'd say.

Now my career had come to a screeching halt. After a few days at home, I started to go nuts. I'd read the paper in the morning, and then couldn't figure out what to do next. I was going through a mid-life crisis, doubting myself and everything I had done. I'd been on a long run. I had kept driving relentlessly forward. Suddenly, it all felt shallow and meaningless.

"What should I do?" I asked Alice. "I've done game shows and kids' shows, and I don't want to do them anymore. I've done talk—I was *good* at talk, and they canceled me."

"Be patient," she said. "You have time. Look around. Get your bearings. You've always landed on your feet. And you will this time, too."

I couldn't hear her. OCD had begun to run my mind. I obsessed on the cancellation of *Biggers and Summers*. The show *had* been great: the marvelous TV and film director Carl Reiner had watched us in action and been blown away. He couldn't believe Sissy and I had just started hosting together. He said it seemed like we'd been together for years. Tom Selleck, Tony Randall, Michael Bolton—they all came on the show as guests, and loved doing it. I had been good at my job. And I had been canned.

I think almost anyone in my situation would have had these thoughts spinning around in his head. But I obsessed on the praise I'd received from Tom Selleck and Carl Reiner. I ran their words over and over in my mind. I couldn't stop. I felt that if I replayed the shows in my mind again and again, somehow I'd fix what was wrong. I'd magically bring back to life what had been taken from me. For hours on end, I'd sit in my favorite chair and visualize the scrolling credits of all the shows I'd hosted. In my mind, I would greet the guests, chat them up, make them feel comfortable, feel the warmth from the audience as they laughed and applauded.

My self-confidence was in meltdown. Was I damaged goods? Could I work again? Maybe I had had my shot. Perhaps the life of show business was simply too volatile, too uncertain.

As it turned out, a big part of my problem was timing. I had come back to L.A. in March of 1996, but January and September are the times in television when shows are traditionally cast. I held my finger up and gauged the wind. Once I realized nothing was going to happen until autumn, I settled down to wait out a long dry summer in the Santa Monica Mountains.

I set about doing what you do in television if you're someone like me who is back in town without work and has missed those hiring windows. You have to constantly remind people who you are and what you do. You take them out for lunch, for drinks, you call them just to say hello—you wine and dine and you have to constantly keep up a cheerful face. Of course, it's exponentially easier to get work in this business if you already have work. If you have work, you have confidence. And people have a sixth sense for someone whose confidence is at an ebb. They smell the fear coming off you. There's nothing you can do to hide it.

In my current state I knew it was risky taking people out to business lunches because I was so emotionally shaky. But I had to send out feelers and let people know I was back in town. So I'd try to kill as many birds with one stone as I could, planning business lunches in places where I knew I was likely to run into show business movers and shakers.

Conversation in L.A. runs like this: "Hi! How are you? What are you up to?" Everyone lives to work here, and work is the first thing on everyone's mind. So chance encounters, running into people at restaurants, can be productive. Everyone knows everyone. It's important that people see you, know you're around.

I wined and dined television executives at Citrus, an upscale restaurant in the bowels of Hollywood. I hosted producers at Hugo's, a Hollywood coffee shop and industry hangout. I took programming people to Nate 'n' Al's, a deli in Beverly Hills. I sprung for the check at The Palm, a steak and lobster joint between Beverly Hills and CBS Television City.

The conversation at these lunches was entirely predictable.

"Gee, what happened at Lifetime?" said the exec.

I told him, trying to sound as upbeat as possible. "Well, they loved the show, but, you know, their programming was moving in another direction. They wanted to cut back on costs."

That's L.A. for you. That's show biz. Even if you get run over by a truck you'd better look on the bright side. You'd better come up smiling.

Inevitably, the conversation rolled around to the question: "What do you want to do now?"

What the hell did he think I wanted to do? Play lead violin in a symphony orchestra?

"I want to do what I do," I said, smiling my best rendition of a Marc Summers A-list smile. "I want to host television shows."

I asked if he was developing anything, and he talked up all the earth-shattering programming he was busy getting off the ground. Isn't that exciting! Isn't that wonderful! I said. What brilliance! Was there a place for me in anything he had in the works? I was sucking up, selling myself like a piece of meat. It's wasn't fun and it wasn't pretty, but it is a big part of this business.

After these lunches, I would drive back on the endless L.A. freeways, cars belching exhaust, the interminable strip malls, the glare of the harsh sun beating down on the concrete that stretched unbroken for mile after mile, the relentless commerce and the unbridled ambition of the world of show business. I thought about the tree-lined street where I'd grown up in genteel Indianapolis, and the boy I had been who made rabbits pop out of hats and dreamt of a life in television—a life that would one day eat him up and spit him out. I came back from those lunches defeated, bloated, the false smile I had plastered on my face making my jaw ache. In hindsight, it's clear that I was overreacting, but at the time, I thought I'd never work again.

My close friends said the cancellation of *Biggers and Summers* was a sign: I needed to make big changes in my life, shake things up, bring in new energy. They urged me to leave my agent and close friend, Richard Lawrence, at Abrahms, Rubaloff, and Lawrence, a successful boutique agency that had handled me for 15 years. So I defected, going over to Ken Lindner and Babette Perry at Ken Lindner and Associates with offices in Century City. Lindner and Associates was another agency that specialized in handling television hosts. The move to my new agents buoyed me momentarily (I've since moved back to the agents who launched me; Richard welcomed me back with a graciousness and lack of resentment that warmed me to my core.)

When I wasn't futilely wining and dining industry executives, I was hanging out at home all day. At first, I was waiting for my belongings to arrive from New York. Then I was unpacking. Then I was neatening.

The stress from being unemployed sent me into an OCD tailspin. I became obsessed with keeping the house straight, and constantly arranged and rearranged paintings, vases, furniture, pillows, curtains, glasses, window blinds, photographs, rug fringes. If it could be moved, adjusted, or rearranged, I was powerless to resist. Every couple of hours I'd have to go through the house, straightening everything, although nothing had been touched since my last round. I'd feel anxiety start to well up. It was like a maddening itch that I couldn't quite scratch. The straightening and restraightening made the itch better for a little while, calmed it, but then it would catch fire again, crawling under my skin, and I'd have to go back and do the whole bloody thing again, moving the cushions by only millimeters, making sure the vase with flowers was placed in the exact center of the table in the foyer.

I didn't clean, dust, or vacuum, as I had when I was a kid. The house was too clean for that, since I had a cleaning woman come in on Mondays and Fridays. If I saw dust on a table I would wipe it off, but the house was basically kept dust-free. So I focused on the symmetry of vases, glasses in the kitchen cabinets, pillows on the couch, food in the refrigerator, the space between the chairs at the dining room table. Everything had to be at just the right angle.

The Monday cleaning lady changed sheets and towels and did the wash and vacuuming. The Friday woman did the hard-core, physical cleaning. She moved everything, picked up pieces of furniture—couches, tables, chairs, beds—and dusted behind them. She left around 3:30 in the afternoon. As soon as she was out the door, I'd go to it. I'd fix everything. The plant on the kitchen table went directly under the middle ceiling lamp, salt and pepper shakers had to be in perfect alignment, the throw rug precisely centered in front of the fridge, the pattern on one couch cushion had to mesh perfectly with the next, the photographs on the mantle had to be just so, the paintings had to be perfectly level. Two hours later everything would be back in its place.

Friday afternoons the kids were away at after-school activities—soccer or theater practice. Alice asked me, "Do you want to come with me to pick up the kids, or do you want to stay here and do your thing around the house?"

You can guess my choice. I knew that I should have gone with her to pick up the kids, but my compulsions came first. As I worked my way through the house, I thought to myself over and over, "I should be spending time with my wife and family." But then I'd think, Oh God, the curtains aren't hanging right. If I just fix it quickly, maybe I can take the kids out for ice cream when they come home.

But, of course, one thing would lead to another. I'd fix the curtain, then notice the photographs on the mantle were out of alignment. I'd fix the photos, then straighten all the paintings on the dining room wall. Then I'd have to straighten all the paintings in the entire house. So when the kids came home, needless to say, there was never time to take them out for ice cream. God forbid they should interrupt me in the midst of my Friday afternoon rounds. When my compulsion was in charge, everything that got in the way of serving it was an interruption—even the needs of my kids and wife.

It was horrible knowing I should be investing energy in the relationships most dear to me. But I was helpless. My helplessness began to make me furious at myself. This kind of self-directed anger is common among OCD sufferers. Our self-knowledge can be devastating—we see that our behavior is ridiculous and self-destructive, yet we can't control it. But it's also one of the blessings of the disorder that we have the sense that our behavior is out of bounds. Unlike people suffering from schizophrenia (another disorder caused by chemical imbalances in the brain), who truly believe their distorted vision of the world, people with OCD do not assume that our obsessions or compulsions make sense or have any bearing on reality. On the *Oprah* show, both Lorrie, who had such acute fears of contamination, and Don, the hoarder, were quick to admit that what they were doing was "out of hand" and "a little bit crazy" but that they had no control over their actions.

I felt the same when Meredith would have friends over, and I would stick my head in her room, "Can I straighten in here a sec?"

Her friends would look at her as if to say, "Is your dad crazy, or what?" Even though I knew teenagers need nothing as much as they need privacy, I couldn't stop.

The embarrassment I caused myself was far outweighed by the embarrassment I caused my daughter, and I knew it. But I couldn't help myself. The most restraint I could muster was to gloss over Meredith's room when she had a friend visiting, instead of giving it the usual detailed straightening.

I became obsessed with the green curtains in the dining room. They had to hit the floor in perfect, even waves, with none of their white lining showing. I'd arrange them, and then, though they hadn't been disturbed, I'd arrange them again. And then a third time. Each time I walked by a carpet I'd straighten it. I spent hours in the kitchen. I wiped and wiped the countertops and straightened the chairs. Our drinking glasses had to be arranged in perfect rows on the cupboard shelves. I should have been trying to write up ideas for shows, to pitch programming. But I was at a creative low. I was usually buzzing with ideas, jotting them down on legal pads. But now I was flat. Empty. My work life was a mess, but if I could make the house perfect, at least something would be right.

I was at a low point in my life. Nothing was developing in my career. When this happens, you always hope that people will find out you've been canceled and call with job offers. Not this time. I felt rejection like a knife.

I started to stay in bed as long as I could each morning. I

didn't want to get up: I didn't have anything to do. A major depression settled over me.

What I had is called "comorbid" depression, meaning a depression that co-existed with my OCD. Two-thirds of obsessive compulsives develop clinical depression at some point in their lives. We suffer classic symptoms of depression: loss of interest and energy, poor concentration, difficulty with sleep, and, in extreme cases, suicidal thoughts. Thankfully, my depression never reached that point. It did, I think, exacerbate my OCD symptoms, which in turn made me even more depressed. A vicious cycle developed, as happens frequently in the lives of depressed people with OCD. It's not always clear if the depression is secondary to the OCD—that is, brought on by the stresses of living with OCD—or a separate illness, labeled "primary" depression. In any event, at the time, the distinction was pointless.

Normally, I'm awake by 5:30 or 6:00 A.M. I spend an hour on the treadmill, watching the early morning news. But now I languished in bed all morning, finally getting up at 11:00 A.M. After staggering to the shower and getting dressed, I would or would not shave, depending on whether I had a depressing business lunch scheduled that day with a producer or agent or lackey whom I thought might help me get work.

I'd hang around the house and finally skulk into my home office. It was set up with a TV and VCR, all the tapes of my appearances on various shows meticulously organized, a big overstuffed chair in one corner, pictures of me with various celebrities hanging on the wall, a private business phone on a spotless desk. Two French doors opened out into a big backyard and the Santa Monica Mountains. The room was quiet, hushed, at the very back of the house. No one went in there except me.

It should have been my haven but now it was my hell. Sitting at the computer was torture. I had no idea what I was going to write. I had vague ideas for show concepts, ideas to pitch. But I told myself that I couldn't begin work until the room was clean. So I killed hours fluffing pillows, straightening furniture, re-arranging videotapes on the shelves.

I should have been taking time off after working like a slave for all those years without a break. I should have been regrouping, looking at my options, planning my next move. But I was incapable of slowing down. A pit of emptiness was opening inside me—a gnawing anxiety I couldn't control. When I unpacked my stuff from New York I found all the material the *Biggers and Summers* producers had given us to prepare for the show we did on OCD. You'd think I would have noticed my behavior and connected it to what I'd learned about OCD from Dr. Hollander on the show that day. I'd admitted to the whole world that I had the disorder—why couldn't I admit it to myself now?

I played the kids a videotape the producers had included of a woman afflicted with OCD straightening her apartment. "I can't believe somebody else does what you do," Meredith said.

Alice and the kids used to look at my compulsions as "eccentricities" and "quirks." They had always felt that cleaning made me happy, so they gave me license to indulge that kind of behavior. They had no idea that I was afflicted by a clinical illness that played havoc with my brain chemistry.

It wasn't until I appeared on *Oprah* that the kids felt self-conscious about having a dad with OCD. After the show, kids in their school would approach them and ask them about their "weird" father. Reporters wanted to interview them on what it was like to have an obsessive compulsive dad. Matthew and Meredith told me they didn't want to be constantly fielding questions about their father, and they asked me to shield them from media people.

"That's your life," Matthew, age 16 at the time, said. "I don't want to be sucked into it."

I respected that, especially because our family dynamic was close, and the kids had never reproached me for my eccentricities. But I do remember one night when I was rearranging the living room, Meredith kept running past me *en route* to Alice, who was helping her with her homework. On one trip she stopped, and said "Dad, please stop doing that. I hate it when you do that."

"Okay," I said as she vanished up the stairs.

I sat down for a minute, feeling lost and confused. I wanted to stop, but anxiety welled up inside me. It grew and grew until I couldn't help myself. I got up and went back to fluffing the couch pillows.

"Dad! Stop!" Meredith had been watching me through the banister rails.

I hung my head. I'd been caught.

At night I watched *David Letterman* and then whatever else happened to come on. I stayed up as late as I could, going to bed around 2:00 A.M. And then it would be 11:00 in the morning again, and Alice would be saying, "Come on; you have to get up; this isn't good for you."

I still didn't consciously realize how driven I was by the disease. I was in denial. I hadn't been officially diagnosed with

OCD, and, although I was pretty sure I had the traits of an obsessive compulsive, I didn't think I needed help. I resisted the thought of taking drugs or the idea that therapy might help me. I still thought I could handle everything myself.

Late one night I was up watching TV. I walked past the oriental rug in our dining room. I knew the fringe was straight, but, as usual, I couldn't help myself—I got down on my hands and knees and started running my fingers along each tassel, placing each on the floor in a perfectly straight line, parallel to all the others. I had to make them perfect. It was a soothing feeling. I knew that if I straightened all the fringe, I'd feel better.

"It's 1:30 in the morning!" Alice's voice, raw and edgy, pierced the stillness. "What are you doing?"

I looked up at her through the darkness. "I have no idea."

There was a long pause.

"Do you have the card of that doctor from the show?" she said. "I think you need to call him."

"I think you're right."

I stood up, went into my office, pulled Dr. Hollander's card from my alphabetized business-card filing box, and placed it by the phone. I resolved to call him as soon as I got up the next morning.

From my work with the Foundation, I now know it's common for OCD sufferers to reach a nadir before seeking treatment. I suppose it's human nature to wait until things get desperate to make changes in our lives. But it doesn't have to be that way. I was terrified of the pills, but, as you'll see in the next chapter, they aren't so bad, and they can make an enormous difference. I think it's important to realize we can't handle the disease on our own. The help lines listed in the back of this book can help you find a doctor or support group in your area. You don't have to go the distance alone. I know that it's doubly hard to address your obsessive compulsive disorder when you're also battling depression. Depression often exists without OCD, but one of my compatriots in the campaign to publicize OCD, Connie Foster, a writer on the disorder, says that OCD is almost always accompanied by depression. Like me, Connie was spurred to seek treatment by her family when she found herself in the throes of a major depression.

"I was overwhelmed with fatigue," she told me. "I wasn't eating. I wanted to sleep all the time. With three children, two horses in the barn, and a business to run, I obviously needed to be on medication. I was so depressed I didn't realize I was depressed. It was my family, my husband and three sons, who sat me down and told me that I needed to get help."

Even though she bottomed out with OCD before seeking treatment, Connie feels that overall her OCD has contributed to the success she's achieved.

"OCD has been more of a help than a hindrance to me," she says. "I wouldn't have accomplished what I accomplished without it. When I sought treatment in 1989, only a few doctors had heard of the disorder. I had to go out of state to Massachusetts General Hospital in Boston for treatment. At that time, Anafranil wasn't approved for use in this country, so I got it from Canada. It helped immediately. First the depression lifted and then the OCD."

When Connie counsels OCD sufferers she likes to remind us and our families that OCD is a chronic illness. "You always have it," she says. "It waxes and wanes. Some days are harder than others. But as we age we tend to live with it more gracefully."

The morning after I resolved to seek help I rolled out of bed before dawn. It was three hours later on the East Coast, and I wanted to catch Dr. Hollander by telephone before his busy day began. I felt acute apprehension. I was worried that I would have to go on medication. If I hadn't promised Alice that I would call I probably wouldn't have followed through.

Alice and the kids were still asleep, and so I felt completely alone in our big dark house. First light was just creeping through the windows. I made my way to my office. I could see the brightness coming up over the jagged spine of the mountains; it was not enough to read by so I flicked on the desk lamp. A small circle of light pooled around Dr. Eric Hollander's card, lying on the desk where I had left it the night before. I felt an overwhelming urge to straighten up the room. Instead, I picked up the card, took a deep breath, and lifted the receiver.

| *nine* |

taking charge

The phone rang twice. "Good morning, Dr. Hollander's office," said the woman who answered.

"Can I speak to Dr. Hollander, please?"

"What is this regarding?"

"My name's Marc Summers." I was nervous. "Dr. Hollander told me to call if I ever needed help. I think I have OCD, and I need help."

After a few minutes, Dr. Hollander's warm voice greeted me. "Marc! What's going on?"

"Hi. Remember that conversation we had in the studio about

my disorder? You said help was available when I needed it. I think I need it."

"Why?"

I took a deep breath. "I straighten all the time," I said.

"What do you mean, all the time?"

I told him about losing *Biggers and Summers* and returning to L.A., about the days spent straightening my immaculate house and getting caught by Meredith, and, finally, about my confrontation with Alice late the night before when she had caught me fixing the fringe on the dining room rug.

"I need to get control of this," I said. "It's running my life. It's hurting my relationship with my wife and kids."

We talked for 30 minutes and then made another appointment to speak by phone in two days. I hung up with the feeling that a burden had at least partially been lifted from me. I didn't have to carry the weight of the disorder alone anymore.

When I spoke to Dr. Hollander again, we talked for an hour. He asked me in detail about my rituals and intrusive thoughts and about when I had first expressed my OCD symptoms. Then he let the bomb drop. "I think you need to go on medication," he said.

I wasn't surprised. We had talked about medication on the show. I knew it was ultimately part of the solution to my problem, but that didn't diminish the anxiety and resistance I felt at the suggestion.

"Why do you say that?" I asked.

Dr. Hollander told me that in his experience, which I knew was extensive, a combination of medication and behavior therapy usually provided the best results for people with OCD. Behavior therapy, he explained, provides lasting benefits by changing the way OCD patients respond to their obsessive thoughts, which eventually leads to a reduction in the thoughts themselves. At first, though, the therapy was likely to increase my feelings of anxiety. Medication, Dr. Hollander said, would take the "edge" off my OCD symptoms, lessening the severity of my anxiety and making the behavior therapy a little easier.

I was foggy on exactly what behavior therapy was, so he went over it on the phone in order to let me know what I was in for. He explained what's called "exposure and response prevention," a regimen familiar to the thousands and perhaps now hundreds of thousands of people who have used it to control their OCD. In exposure and response prevention, an OCD patient is encouraged to face his fears, to expose himself to the very things that induce his obsessive thoughts. A person with contamination fears might be asked to touch a T-shirt he considers germ-covered. That's the exposure part. In the response prevention part, the patient is asked to resist, for a certain length of time, doing the compulsive rituals he would normally do to ease his anxiety-provoking obsessive thoughts. The patient who has touched the "germ-covered" T-shirt and is terrified he's been contaminated must now resist his urge to run to the bathroom sink and scrub his hands. At first the OCD patient is asked to resist for only a short time, and then gradually to do so for longer and longer. As it becomes clear to the patient that he hasn't gotten sick and that nothing bad has happened because he hasn't washed his hands, the power that his obsessive fear of contamination has over him begins, bit by bit, to diminish.

Dr. Hollander suggested we begin behavior therapy by using

the ferocious compulsion I had to straighten after the cleaning woman left on Fridays. Our goal was to help me begin to recognize that if I didn't rearrange the house after she left, nothing would happen. No one would get hurt.

"Do you think you can wait five minutes after she leaves before you begin straightening?" he asked.

"Yes," I said.

"10 minutes?"

"Yes."

"15 minutes?"

"Don't push it."

We decided I'd wait five minutes that Friday after Nati left, and that as the weeks and months passed I would increase the time I resisted acting on my compulsions from five minutes to an hour. This process, Dr. Hollander explained, might actually begin to correct the biochemical processes in my brain. Psychiatric researchers have only recently discovered that behavior therapy seems to have much the same effect on the brain as OCD medications: through therapy, the different brain regions that are hyperactive and "locked" together in OCD patients (the orbital frontal cortex, the basal ganglia, and the thalamus) become less hyperactive and less "locked." Dr. Hollander told me, unable to conceal his excitement, that this is one of the most exciting discoveries ever made in psychiatry.

It is well known that therapy can change patients' moods, understandings, views of life, and behavior without the help of medication. For a long time psychiatrists have suspected it can change patients' brains as well, but they've never been able to prove it. Using imaging devices that provide pictures of brain activity, it has recently become possible to see how the hyperactive, locked regions of the brain become normal during treatment with behavior therapy. It's the first (and only) evidence of therapy resulting in a specific change in the brain.

Dr. Hollander asked if I was going to be in New York any time soon.

"I can be."

"Why don't you come in and we'll talk some more?"

When I told Alice that my first OCD treatment was to wait five minutes after the cleaning woman had left before I started straightening on Friday afternoon, she smiled.

"I'll believe it when I see it," she said.

I saw she was teasing me. "Oh, ye of little faith!" I said.

"I know you can do it, Marc. You can do anything when you put your mind to it."

That Friday at 3:30, after our front door clicked shut behind Nati, I stood in our kitchen, eyes closed, hands clenched. I felt the insidious anxiety gripping my belly and chest. I was short of breath. I checked and rechecked my watch, pacing through the house, trying to keep my eyes away from couch pillows that were slightly off-kilter, the dining room curtains that didn't hang quite right.

I made it through the five minutes—barely. As soon as my allotted time was up, I began frantically straightening and rearranging. The waiting had been torture, but I felt stronger afterward, as though whatever it was that had a stranglehold on my psyche had loosened its grip somewhat.

A week later, I flew to New York to see Dr. Hollander. I stayed at the RIHGA Royal, my hotel of choice at the time. It was a great place to run into people in the industry. There tend to be hot hotels for celebrities in New York that change every four or five years, and in my business, every chance encounter can lead to work. In television, you must constantly position yourself to run into people, to be seen—until you reach a certain level, that is. Stars, at that level, crave anonymity.

I didn't choose hotels only because there were celebrities in the lobby. I also factored in my need for cleanliness. The RIHGA was a new hotel, and the staff kept the place spotless. I have a terrible time in hotels. I never walk barefoot anywhere but in my own house. I carry a pair of flip-flops to use in the shower when I travel, and I have a highly evolved system for showering and getting dressed so that my bare feet never touch the floor. I take off all my clothes, except my socks, while sitting on the bed. One at a time, I slip my feet into my flip-flops. I lay clean socks on the bed—only on the sheets, of course; *never* on the bedspread. (Who knows *what's* been on the bedspread?) Then I get in the shower. I have a phobia about the shower curtain, which can't be completely closed when I'm behind it (I don't know if it's claustrophobia or the sense that the curtain is dirty). This means that water inevitably sprays on the floor, so I put down plenty of towels beforehand. I wash my feet one at a time, slipping first one and then the other out of its flip-flop. I can't let any part of my body touch the shower curtain or the bathroom wall, so I stand, balanced precariously, on one leg like a flamingo.

The night before my meeting with Dr. Hollander I felt my life was about to change. I was still struggling to accept that my need for help was not an admission of defeat or a sign of weakness, but actually an indication of strength, growth, maturity. We're conditioned in this culture, especially as men, to think we have carry our load alone. We think that if we can't handle it on our own there's something wrong with us, something lacking.

Not only am I an OCD sufferer and a man to boot, I also have a type A personality. I like being in charge. I prefer not only to host but also to be involved with writing and producing my shows whenever possible. My need for control was so intense that I needed to go into hypnotherapy in 1987 to cope with my fear of flying. When in an airplane I was terrified because my life was in the pilot's hands, which meant that I had no control. Sometimes when we hit turbulence I would even start to cry. In 1986, being the host of *Double Dare* meant that I was suddenly airborne several times a month, since we shot the show at a variety of locations. It was unbearable. I knew I needed help, and I finally confessed my fear of flying to my doctor. He said hypnosis would help.

"You can't hypnotize me," I said. I thought I was too much in control of myself.

"Oh yes, I can!"

He was right. I lay down on his examination table, and he turned down the lights. He started talking in a soft, soothing voice, and in no time at all I was deep in a trance.

Dr. Hollander has since told me that one of the reasons he thought I'd make a good candidate for behavior therapy was the success I'd had with hypnotherapy. It indicated that I could follow directions and was motivated to change. He said hypnosis had been tried on people with OCD, but it had been largely ineffectual: less than 15 percent of patients showed signs of improvement.

Hypnotherapy helped my fear of flying, but I must admit I'm still queasy on planes. It takes a long time for guys like me to realize that we don't have all the answers, that we need help, that we can't control life. That night in my hotel room I lay awake wondering if I was surrendering a core part of myself by ceding control of my psyche to someone else. I didn't suspect that by sharing my fears, instead of insisting that I had all the answers and was completely self-sufficient and independent, I was about to take charge of my life for the first time.

The next morning I walked from midtown Manhattan up Fifth Avenue. It was a breezy spring morning. White clouds raced low and fast over the glittering tops of buildings. Kids skipped down the steps to the Central Park Zoo. Nannies pushed baby carriages, and elderly women leaned on walkers, guided by nurses in starched uniforms. I passed the Metropolitan Museum of Art and the Guggenheim, finally coming to 98th Street and Mt. Sinai Hospital, where Dr. Hollander has his office.

I took a seat in a small waiting room and nervously flipped through a magazine. Dr. Hollander soon appeared. We shook hands, and he led me into his office, a large room with a view out over Central Park.

I smiled to myself at the clutter of the office, so unlike my own with its pristine surfaces. There were tons of books strewn all over the floor, shelves, and desks. I noted several that Dr. Hollander himself had written on OCD. It looked like a professor's office, not in the least pretentious. Dr. Hollander was dressed in one of what I came to recognize as his typical off-the-rack rumpled suits. His manner was warm, and I was again struck by his youth.

I reported my attempt to resist my compulsion to clean that previous Friday.

"You might be able to get better on behavior therapy alone," he told me, "but I recommend you try medication."

I hedged. "I don't want to rely on pills for the rest of my life."

"It's your decision."

There was a long pause. "As much as I hate pills, I hate more how I've been feeling," I finally said.

When I left Dr. Hollander that day I felt great; all the discomfort and anxiety had been drained from me. I marched, prescription in hand, to a pharmacy on Madison Avenue. I strolled around the Upper East Side while the prescription was being filled. The pills might make me better, but I still resisted the thought that I might have to rely on them.

After an hour wandering the streets, I reentered the pharmacy and emerged with my vial of Luvox.

Fluvoxamine (Luvox) is one of several medications approved by the Food and Drug Administration for treating OCD and was first approved to treat children and adolescents. Luvox is the drug that worked for me; other, equally effective drugs used to treat OCD include clomipramine (Anafranil), fluoxetine (Prozac), paroxetine (Paxil), and sertraline (Zoloft). There are also several other promising drugs awaiting FDA approval. In his office, Dr. Hollander had explained how the medications work. You'll remember that neurons release serotonin, among other neurotransmitters, which carry impulses across synapses. OCD drugs are known as serotonin reuptake inhibitors because they block, or inhibit, the "reuptake pumps" whose job it is to collect serotonin from the synapse and bring it back to the neuron that released it.

Blocking these reuptake pumps allows the serotonin levels in the brain of an OCD patient to rise, which, after a number of weeks, changes the sensitivity of serotonin receptors. This restores balance to the serotonin system and normalizes the hyperactive and locked regions of the brain that had me on a continual feel-anxious, must-straighten-fringe loop. Almost all of these drugs affect only serotonin and no other neurotransmitters, and they are therefore known as *selective* serotonin reuptake inhibitors. All five OCD drugs are also effective in treating depression, which Dr. Hollander pointed out was often useful, since so many OCD sufferers also suffer from depression. Some people respond better to some medications than others, and side effects vary from person to person. It can take three months before a medication shows its full effect, and it often takes trial and error to find the right medication. But I was lucky: Dr. Hollander's first choice was right for me.

I figured I'd go on meds for a few weeks, get cured, and get off them again. I flew back to L.A. and resumed my life: looking for work and straightening fringe. I checked in with Dr. Hollander once a week. I made progress with behavior therapy, which wasn't as difficult as I thought it would be. The Friday after my visit to New York I extended the time I waited to start straightening up after the cleaning woman left to 10 minutes. The week after, I waited 15 minutes. I was taking baby steps, but at least I saw progress. Other sufferers of OCD have a harder time of it. They find that behavior therapy initially increases their anxiety level, and so they stop the therapy before it has a chance to work. Behavior therapy is not instantaneous and it takes effort.

My resistance to behavior therapy came when Dr. Hollander asked me to wait 40 minutes before straightening. Half an hour had been manageable, but waiting any longer than that, for some mysterious reason, sent me into a panic. The sight of the mussed fringe of the dining room rug made me nervous. I tried to watch television to distract myself. But I couldn't sit still. Dr. Hollander suggested that if I began to cave in to my compulsions I should leave the house, get in the car, and drive away. But that would have been an admission of defeat. Just as I always have to win when I play Monopoly with my children, I was damned if I would "lose" to my OCD. My perfectionism extended to behavior therapy. I had to be the best patient possible. So I stayed and suffered. Hollander told me that he has treated other OCD patients who are hypervigilant, obsessed with how well they respond to treatment.

For most OCD sufferers, family participation is necessary for successful treatment. The OC Foundation believes optimal treatment includes medication, behavior therapy, family education, and the right kind of family support. On the one hand, it's common for families to get sucked into OCD rituals because they want to ease the anxiety of their loved one. Parents of kids with contamination OCD often do their children's laundry repeatedly, performing their children's rituals for them. On the other hand, there are families who become enraged at the obsessive compulsive sufferer's strange behavior. They scream at him or her: "Just stop it!" They blame the person with OCD for his or her behavior.

Neither approach is productive, and the pattern my family fell into wasn't, either. Although they didn't actively participate in my straightening and ordering compulsions, Alice and the kids did cater to my idiosyncrasies. Because I didn't like having people in the house, we had very few guests, and my OCD made my family neater than they otherwise would have been and even somewhat uncomfortable in their own home. My disorder curtailed all our freedom.

In the beginning of my treatment, the producers of *Dateline NBC* asked if they could come into my house and film my obsessive compulsive life. I was making progress with behavior therapy, but my medication hadn't kicked in yet, and I felt far too embarrassed about my compulsions to let cameras in the house to film me. After Nati left, although I was up to a full hour before straightening, I still, inevitably, ended up down on my hands and knees, running my fingers through that carpet fringe.

The *Dateline* appearance had been suggested by Ketchum Communications, a public relations firm hired as part of the OC Foundation's campaign to promote public awareness of the disorder. *Dateline* had already done a piece on a woman with OCD who was much more severely afflicted than I was. She had strong contamination fears. She didn't like dirt, and I remember that *Dateline* shot her walking barefoot through dirt. It made me wince.

Dateline wanted to revisit the disorder. The producers liked the fact that I was a celebrity and I had a tie-in with *Double Dare*. "Neatness freak slimed for a living" made a good lead for a story that would focus on what we hoped would be my successful treatment.

I was nervous about doing national publicity on OCD. When I agreed to work on behalf of the Foundation, I never thought I'd be doing national shows like *Dateline* or *Oprah*. I pictured myself doing radio spots for a local station in Des Moines, not opening my house to national TV. I told the *Dateline* producers to give me a few more months, and we scheduled filming for that fall. (After the *Dateline* piece, some people actually asked me if I did it for notoriety, to increase my visibility. People in this business are relentlessly cynical. The truth is that I never thought that way.)

Dr. Hollander suggested that I go to group therapy sessions at a behavior therapy clinic for OCD sufferers organized by the neuropsychiatric division of the UCLA Medical Center. He thought that being around people who were successfully treating their OCD through behavior therapy might inspire me. I thought I'd give the clinic a shot, even though I had the same resistance to group therapy that I'd had when I sought Dr. Hollander's help in the first place and went on medication: it was hard admitting to myself I still wasn't in full control, that OCD still had a grip on me.

This admission was especially tormenting with the *Dateline* piece fast approaching, because I couldn't imagine being less than completely cured on television. But I was committed to the treatment process. I was determined to do whatever it took to get better.

The group was run by Courtney Jacobs, a psychiatrist in her thirties with a professional New York manner. Her office was a couple of blocks from UCLA's Westwood campus. The members of my group of OCD patients would gather in the waiting room while Jacobs finished up with a private patient. We would sit there, with only our OCD in common, not saying a word. It was creepy. Four to seven people came to each weekly Thursday night session. The members of my group were a shy, eccentric bunch. Most had trouble talking about the disorder, but I had no trouble at all. Once I was finally diagnosed and began to receive treatment, I never hesitated to discuss the disorder or my symptoms. After all those years of internal suffering, I was through with keeping secrets.

A 17-year-old kid who reminded me of my son Matt drove from San Diego every week to attend the group session. He barely said a word. I thought of myself at 17, how much more outgoing I was than this poor kid who sat staring at the floor and didn't seem able to tell us about his symptoms.

A Hispanic man in the group had severe contamination fears, which was particularly unfortunate because he made his living as a phlebotomist. His job was to draw blood from people. Although he wore gloves, he was convinced that he was exposing himself to viruses. I told him he should look for another job. But he said he wanted to work in the medical field and someday hoped to become a doctor. It was heartbreaking.

One young woman in the group was a writer. She was very open, even flamboyant, about her disorder. She was a hoarder, and her apartment was filled to the brim with junk. She loved to talk about how many medications she was taking and how many different doctors were looking after her case. She went on and on about it. One session I asked her, "Are your doctors talking to each other? Do they know what medications the other ones are prescribing for you?" She said they did, but I didn't believe her.

The sessions involved going around the room, each of us

telling the group what kind of week we'd had and how our behavior therapy had gone. This was the first time that I'd seen, up
close and personal, the spectrum of people with the disorder. I
saw how broad it was, and how the severity of symptoms varied
from one person to another. I felt lucky that my own symptoms
were relatively mild and not as disabling as those of some of the
other people in the group.

Very soon, the sessions became painful for me. I would sit
there during the frequent tortured periods of silence and think,
"Why am I here?" Someone, usually the flamboyant girl, would
pierce the silence with a lament of how hard it was to have OCD,
and I would think, "Why are *any* of you here? You don't even
want to talk about ways to get better!" Maybe they just hadn't gotten to that stage yet, but I felt unforgiving; my mission was to go
in, get better, and get out.

By the third meeting, I was exasperated. I felt the others were
just coming to therapy to feel sorry for themselves.

"You guys don't want to get better," I told them. "You just
want to complain." There was a silence in the room. "You can
take control of this, but if you don't want to get better, you won't."

No one said a word. That was the last time I went to group
therapy. I talked to Dr. Hollander about the decision to stop going. He said he had hoped I'd find positive role models at UCLA:
people combating the illness successfully. But, given the situation of silence and stasis in the group, we agreed it was probably
a waste of time.

One positive experience did come from my visits to the clinic
at UCLA. The group leader, Courtney Jacobs, worked on an OCD
children's ward at the UCLA Medical Center. She told the par-

ents I was in her behavior therapy group, and the parents invited me to speak to their kids. I became friends with a boy named Trent who had been hospitalized for a month because his obsessive thoughts had him convinced that his family was contaminated. Of course, he knew they weren't, but his OCD was so overwhelming that he couldn't function at home. He wouldn't let his family near him. If they touched his jacket, he'd have to throw it out. If they touched his sneakers, he had to get new sneakers. He was a fabulous kid who was fighting his symptoms valiantly and who desperately wanted to get better.

I recently talked to Trent's parents, who told me that he is now in his own apartment, working and living with roommates. He's talking about getting ready to go to college. Life is going well.

During the time I was going to the clinic, Dr. Hollander had me on 50 milligrams of Luvox a day. I didn't notice any improvement, and I gained five pounds in the first month of treatment. Extremely concerned, I called Dr. Hollander. I photograph heavy on television anyway, and I was afraid additional weight would hurt my career. But I started to carefully watch what I ate, and the weight gain stopped. Medications for OCD are miracle workers, but, like all medications, they have side effects. This is why you'll frequently see people going on and off them. It's a balancing act—the dosage against the side effects, and how much you want to get better against how the medication makes you feel.

I was frustrated when I noticed nothing but extra pounds after my initial Luvox regimen. There was no change in my desire to straighten and control. So Dr. Hollander recommended I break a pill in half and try 75 milligrams daily. That's when I started to notice a difference. Suddenly, I didn't have the need to straighten as much. It was the strangest feeling. For my whole life I had felt the need to clean. But now, after Nati left, I didn't need to get down on my hands and knees to straighten fringe. I felt jubilant. But I also wondered if there was something wrong with me. I'd trained myself to think that compulsive straightening was a healthy, normal activity. It was the rest of the slobbish world that was demented.

In the early phases of treatment, before the medication had kicked in, *Dateline* had been to my house to film my Friday afternoon post-Nati cleaning binges. They filmed me moving through the house with manic energy, rearranging dishes in the dishwasher, tilting mirrors until they were perfectly level, and, of course, straightening the fringe on the dining room rug.

"The fringe drives me the most crazy," I told them.

I straightened for 57 minutes, with TV cameras following my every move.

"57 minutes," Alice scoffed later. "That's nothing, Marc. You used to go on for almost two hours."

Later *Dateline* filmed me and Sara James, the reporter covering the story, watching footage of my straightening binge that Friday afternoon. Watching myself I felt deeply ashamed. I saw just how sick I was. How driven. I looked away from the screen as I saw myself entering Meredith's room, an adolescent girl's haven, and asking her if I could tidy up.

When Sara James asked how I felt watching this footage, I nearly broke down.

"It upsets me," I choked out. "It doesn't make me happy."

Even now I wince to think of it.

Altogether the NBC crew must have filmed 8 or 9 hours of

Marc Summers battling OCD, most of it in my house. I would hate to have been the one to edit all that. The crew was sensitive to my family's needs, conscious of being in our space. They were nervous, too; careful never to let their cameras hit the walls. If they had, and a single black scuff mark had appeared, they knew I would have to haul out paint and brush and get rid of that spot.

I'm still amazed that I let people into my house to film such a private part of my life. It has helped people, though: colleges and high schools all over the country use the *Dateline* piece to teach about OCD. I'm not saying it was easy for me. In the middle of filming, I had second thoughts.

"I'm not sure this is a good idea." I said to the producer, Fred Rothenberg.

"This is very good thing," he countered. "You're helping a lot of people."

Of course, he had to say that to me: he couldn't afford to lose me mid-way into the filming. But his words were genuine. I wanted to follow through. The thought that I was helping people continued to motivate me.

Dateline wanted to shoot me in a session with Dr. Hollander, to give viewers some background on our relationship. We flew to New York so they could shoot an hour-long session of the two of us talking in his office, of which only moments appeared in the final cut. That's television for you.

Spring turned into summer, and I still hadn't found work. But things were looking up. One of my best friends, Mark Maxwell-Smith, had developed a new game show, *Majority Rules,* and sold it to Dreamworks SKG, the charismatic start-up company founded by Steven Spielberg, Jeffrey Katzenberg, and David Geffen.

The idea of the show was to poll 99 audience members on questions that ranged from who had the worst hair on television to whether Martin Luther King's birthday should be a public holiday. If you voted with the majority you got to enter the next round. The polling eliminated contestants until two came onstage for an opportunity to win $5,000.

Mark, a fellow magician, was one of the first people I had met in L.A. We'd worked together writing *Truth or Consequences* in 1974. He had since become a prolific producer of daytime television and had been extremely helpful to my career, always believing in my talent and helping me find work. Mark was involved with the *Majority Rules* hiring process, but it was Katzenberg and a tight circle of people around him who made the decisions.

Dreamworks had auditioned literally scores of people, looking for a host. At first they didn't think I was famous enough to audition for them, but Mark got them to take a look at me. After my long dry period without work, I was under a lot of pressure. I was a veteran. I'd been around the block; I was in my mid-forties, and I needed this show. Driving to the NBC studios in Burbank I wondered if I would be perceived as a has-been. When *Double Dare* became a hit, the show generated lots of attention. I was asked to host programs like *Couch Potatoes* without even an audition. The same was true when I hosted the twentieth anniversary show for *NOVA* on PBS. But now I was back in the position of proving myself all over again.

Mark had been feeding me information for months, keeping me abreast of the show's development. Dreamworks had gone down a list of literally 100 people, looking for the right host. Each time they rejected a prospect, Mark said to them, "Why don't you try Marc Summers? Let me bring him in." But they wanted a star, someone with big-name recognition. After months of rejects, they finally said, okay, let's take a look at Summers.

I wasn't nervous on the way to the audition because I didn't think I had a shot. This was a good thing because I kept telling myself that if I was nervous I was going to screw up. I knew there would be a live audience at the audition, which, in fact, would be a run-through of an actual show. I'm just going to keep doing what I do, I thought. I'm a touchy-feely kind of host. I throw my arm around contestants' shoulders; I ask about their families.

The audition went extremely well. I felt completely comfortable on the stage, totally in control. I got in a few good lines, and the rapport between me and the audience was strong. I knew I was right for the show.

Mark was upbeat. He said the inner circle was due to meet a couple of days after the audition to make a decision. He'd let me know what the outcome was.

But when the inner circle met they couldn't come to a consensus. Katzenberg said the show was called *Majority Rules,* so they should take a vote, and whoever won would be host.

I won the vote. I had a job, a plum job. Except that they wanted to hire me and start taping shows even as they continued to look for another more famous host who would then take over. But Mark refused to let them bring me on the show under those conditions.

"I told those guys that even if you had not been a friend, I would never have set you up in that way," Mark said to me, recounting his battles with Katzenberg and Co. "There was silence after I said this. Then the same guy who said we should keep looking for someone else while you hosted the show said 'Okay. The job is his to lose.'" Meaning that I had the job until I screwed up or proved I couldn't handle it.

It often strikes people outside the industry as odd that a company as classy as Dreamworks wanted to produce game shows. But there's a ton of money to be made in the games. If you hit it big with a *Wheel of Fortune* or a *Jeopardy*, it's like you're printing money. The shows don't cost anything to produce: one set, a host's salary, and that's it. The costs are fixed. If your ratings are good, you drown in money. That's why Dreamworks was involved.

I ended up co-hosting the show with Arthel Neville, zydeco musician Arthur Neville's daughter. The pay was great. I never saw Spielberg, but Katzenberg was involved in everything. He was a total perfectionist . . . something I could really relate to!

We ran the show in two test markets: New Orleans and Phoenix. It came in first in its ratings in New Orleans and third in Phoenix, but when we shopped it around for syndication, no one picked it up. Dreamworks promptly canceled the show, took a two million dollar bath, and I was out on the street again, looking for work.

I was shaken, but a different man from the one I'd been a year ago who'd had no confidence after losing a job and ended up compulsively straightening fringe at 1:30 in the morning. I felt relaxed. My whole demeanor was different. By the winter of 1998 when the show was canceled, I was so relaxed that I was worried my television persona would be affected. I thought viewers might see a Marc Summers with diminished energy. My producers had to keep reassuring me that I was the same man on camera I had always been. But internally I felt completely different.

The change hadn't come all at once. Through the late summer and fall, my compulsions to straighten, to read signs over and over, and to make endless lists in my head would still show themselves from time to time. And I felt a chronic recurrence of anxiety. When Dr. Hollander upped my dosage to 100 milligrams, the effect was incredible. The desire to arrange and rearrange disappeared. The desire to have everything in its place just vanished. The anxious hum that had buzzed in the back of my brain all my life was suddenly silent. That silence felt to me like a miracle.

It was at this point that *Dateline* met me with cameras rolling at the door of my home and filmed me as I walked inside. They had set up all their equipment in my living room, a room which was *never* used. That room, like all the living rooms in all the houses I had ever lived in, was a museum piece, perfect, immaculate. When we had company over, we sat in the den because the living room was out of bounds. But *Dateline* had rearranged all the furniture, set up cameras, monitors, lights, run cables and wires everywhere, and generally made a mess. They had turned my pristine environment into seething chaos.

This was the acid test. Sara James and her crew watched closely to see if I'd buckle. But I was actually able to sit down in my invaded sanctum as the cameras rolled. I won't say it didn't bother me, that I didn't have the urge to rip the place apart and put it back together to my liking, but the urge was distant, not pressing; a faint, inconsequential echo of its former self.

I felt good. It was a nice closure to my treatment process. I knew the crew so well that I ordered in sandwiches for everyone. We all sat around laughing about how afraid they'd been to eat in my home at the beginning, for fear of spilling anything; how they'd been afraid to sit down, practically afraid to breathe. Now as crumbs and chips littered the carpet, I barely noticed.

ten

waging war and winning

[Until OCD] no other disorder in the history of medicine has ever experienced such explosive growth in scientific understanding that has led to such a revolution in how it has been viewed: from regarded as rare to recognized as common; from presumed psychological to proven neurobiological; from written off as hopeless to accepted as one of the most responsive of all mental disorders.

—Ian Osborn, M.D.,
Tormenting Thoughts and Secret Rituals

When *Majority Rules* went off the air, I found myself pounding the pavement again, looking for work. That doesn't mean quite the same thing in L.A. as it does in New York City. In L.A., no one walks anywhere, least of all to work. So, for me, "pounding the pavement" meant cruising around to meetings and lunches in my SUV, a Toyota 4Runner, in air-conditioned comfort, cell phone at my side.

I had my confidence back. I had been working at Dream-works, which had cachet, an aura of power and class. When the company's founders, Spielberg, Katzenberg, and Geffen, had first started out, the industry thought they were invincible; that everything they touched would turn to gold. Hollywood is a strange town: there was some glee and not-so-discreet snickering when Dreamworks' syndicated television division, which had developed *Majority Rules*, went belly-up. Nonetheless, even early on, when some of Dreamworks' projects were floundering, the magic and charisma attached to its principals' names counted for a lot in a town where image is everything.

During this period, I acted as a spokesperson for people with obsessive compulsive disorder, making appearances across the country. I was also working for the Game Show Network, spearheading the Network's Coast to Coast Search for a Host. It was a marketing project designed to boost the Network's visibility. I'd arrive with a Network PR person in a city like Cincinnati, Cleveland, or Minneapolis and work the press, giving prearranged interviews for local radio and television stations, spreading the word that Marc Summers had come to town looking for the next Bob Barker or Pat Sajak.

The following day we would build a mini-set for a television game show in a shopping center or a nightclub. The would-be Barkers and Sajaks came to audition. Some had some broadcasting experience, but most had never been in front of a camera. They were librarians, schoolteachers, accountants, truck drivers. I was the master of ceremonies as we ran them through a mock game show in front of a live audience. Sometimes the performances would be surprisingly good. But, more often, our would-be hosts would sweat and stammer through the run-throughs. A group of people from the Game Show Network flew in and acted as judges along with local celebrities. The winners of the local auditions competed against each other for the prize of hosting a nationally televised game show for a week.

The job was fun: I felt like Ed McMahon, fronting a company. As always, going on radio and television fulfilled my craving to perform, to be on the air. And the money was good. But I wasn't doing a television show, which was where I really wanted to be. At other times in my life, the stress from not having a show of my own might have sent me into an OCD tailspin. But the medication and behavior therapy were working well, and for the first time in my life, I was free of rituals and anxious thoughts. The distress I felt about not having a show didn't have the same gnawing quality that it had had in the past. It didn't lead to repetitive circular thoughts, my mind going round and round like a rat in its cage running on a wheel for hours on end.

I was going to auditions, meeting people, working to develop ideas for shows. But it was touch and go. Nothing jelled. Then, in August, I auditioned to host *Hollywood Squares.* Sean Perry was heading the show. I didn't want to do another game show, but *Hollywood Squares* was a plum, a classic which, in its heyday in the late 1960s, had been about entertainment, not prizes. Those were the days when Charlie Weaver, Wally Cox, and Paul Lynde sat in the Squares. Lynde sat in the center, and he drew in viewers. He was quick, sharp, perpetually dissatisfied, nasal, almost sneering, and his outrageous sense of humor let him get away with some very politically incorrect answers. Once he was asked the question, "Paul, you walk into your house. The walls are brown, the ceiling is brown, the floors are brown. What happened?"

"The maid exploded," he answered.

Back then, game shows still had importance. Anyone who was big on television played *Hollywood Squares,* and the show also drew film stars like Henry Fonda and Glenn Ford.

Hollywood Squares, like the other classic game shows—*Family Feud, Wheel of Fortune*—is a perennial. It went off the air only to be recast and resurrected. When King World, the biggest, most powerful syndication company in the business, decided to bring *Squares* back, there was a lot of buzz around the show. It was an opportunity for a host to have a high degree of visibility. That's why my agent, Babette, was excited when she called me during our family's vacation in Hawaii.

"Perry wants you to audition for *Squares,*" she said. "Tomorrow."

I was feeling really good at this point. On family vacations in the past I would have been on the phone half the time, wheeling and dealing, taking care of business. My family understood that this was who I was, and that my efforts made it possible for us to have a comfortable life. But on this vacation, I checked my voice mail only once a day, and I only made a couple of calls a day, just to take care of urgent business. Given the new me, you can imagine how torn I felt when Babette called.

"Fly home," she said.

I thought about it for a moment. Even a year earlier, I would have jumped on the first plane back to L.A.

"If they want me bad enough, they can wait," I told Babette. "I'll be home in a couple of days."

"If that's what you want to do," she said. "But I can't guarantee anything. You may be cut out of the auditions."

"Screw it," I said. "I'll take the chance."

For once, I felt unwilling to part with my family and put work first.

As it turned out, I wasn't cut out of the audition, and I showed up at the appointed time, rested and tanned. It took place in a little office building on Cahuenga Boulevard, near the NBC studios in Burbank. It was the first of three auditions, all of which went well. I was dealing from a position of strength: I wasn't going to run when they whistled. My attitude was that if I got the show, I got it; if not, fine.

I was hired in October. I got a nice fat chunk of money on signing, and then additional funds for *not* working, since shows for syndication are cast a year ahead of the time they're due to air. Rehearsals for the show weren't due to start until the following summer. *Hollywood Squares* didn't want me taking another job in the interim, so they paid me not to work. I still did my OCD speaking engagements, but, basically, I was hanging out. And I felt relaxed! I wasn't running around every minute of every day, and I still felt calm. I spent time with my family. Saw friends. Enjoyed life. Looked forward to the summer when I'd start working again.

Then I was fired from *Squares* in March of 1998, even before they had taped any shows. A new management team had come in and cleaned house. Out with the old and in with the new. Welcome, once again, to show business! By this point I knew that I would never feel secure in the entertainment industry. Never.

The reality of show business is that even though you have a

contract, it doesn't mean anything. Contracts are never in favor of the talent; they're always in favor of the network or the producers. It's a scary business: yes doesn't necessarily mean yes, as I learned my first week in L.A., when I was promised a job that was snatched from me hours later by the very guy who had given me the lead.

After I was released from *Squares* in March of 1998, my work with Porter Novelli, a PR firm that coordinates my speaking appearances at OCD conferences with groups such as the OC Foundation, the National Mental Health Association, Freedom from Fear, and others, became increasingly important to me. On the day preceding a conference I would do radio and TV spots, explaining OCD and its common symptoms. "Come attend a free seminar tonight. Talk to experts in the field," I'd say on the air. I was always amazed at the turnout: we'd fill ballrooms.

I would speak for 30 minutes, capsulizing my life story. After I was done, medical experts would discuss childhood OCD, the serotonin system, why the disorder occurs, and some of the treatments available. Then we'd open the discussion to questions. I'd go down into the audience with a microphone, keeping the show rolling. It kept me sharp with my career skills: working any big audience is a lot like hosting a television show. The OC Foundation organized events like these in six cities last year. This year we'll do eight.

But it's hard to get up and tell my story over and over and over again at Foundation meetings. It gets harder and harder. I feel played-out sometimes, like I'm repeating myself; I want to move on. It's difficult to talk about my symptoms, to keep the disorder in the forefront of my life. I often just don't want to deal with it. I want it to go away. But keeping it in my face has been as important in my war against OCD as medication or behavior therapy. It renews my vow not to fall back into my old OCD behaviors. By leading conversations about the disorder every four to six weeks, I stay on track. I tell people about what I've been through, and in doing so I'm also reminding myself that you can get better, but you have to *want* to get better.

Very few people are ever fully "cured" of OCD. I expect a continuous battle to keep my symptoms at bay for the rest of my life. It's a day-to-day war, and most days I'm winning. I like to say that I'm 80 percent cured. When I'm feeling good and fully employed, OCD is number 17 on my list of things I have to worry about. But occasionally, when I don't have enough going on, when I'm not busy and occupied with my career and family, things get hairy.

Even after undergoing intensive therapy, relapses are common for OCD sufferers. A relapse happens when you're on the path to success; after taking three steps forward, you suddenly find you've been kicked two steps back. When I was speaking in New York recently, I met a woman suffering from OCD who worked in a hardware store in Fort Wayne, Indiana. One of her jobs was to mix paint. She had paint on her hands all the time. You can imagine how she felt: her job was pure torture for her. When she went on medication, her symptoms disappeared, but she wanted to get off medication quickly. As soon as she did, her symptoms came back in full force.

My own relapse came last summer, when, without warning,

my symptoms came rushing back. My mother-in-law had just died. Matthew left for his first year of college, and I knew that even when he came back for weekends and vacations, things wouldn't be the same. A part of my life seemed to have died with my mother-in-law (we had been very close), and another part of me died when Matthew left. I wasn't prepared to lose him, even if it was the normal separation that occurs when children become adults. To top it off we had just moved into a new house in Calabasas. The upkeep on the 6,000-square-foot palace had been enormous, and, with Matthew gone and Meredith never home, it seemed ridiculous to have so much space.

Several months before the move, I had taken myself off medication without consulting Dr. Hollander. One day I just went cold turkey. I felt I had the disorder licked, and I suppose I was like many other people when I decided to go off medication. I didn't like the thought of being dependent on a pill. I wanted to feel that my body was functioning naturally. Subconsciously, perhaps, I thought that as long as I was medicated I officially *had* OCD: by stopping the medication I would be cured.

Unfortunately, I soon learned the fallacy of this magical thinking. For a while everything was fine. I felt I had the disorder under control. I was not as stressed, rushed, or pressured as I had been in the past without medication. When I started to obsess on cleaning, organizing, and my various rituals, I was able to just walk away, to leave the dirty dishes in the sink, the fringe of the dining room rug messed up, the pillows asymmetrical on the couch. I was damned proud of myself.

I didn't know it at the time, but going off medication abruptly, as I did, is a dangerous maneuver. You're supposed to wean yourself off the medication under careful supervision. You need to pick the right time, when your life is stable. Going off medication suddenly can lead to what's called SSRI discontinuation syndrome. This syndrome can produce vivid dreams or nightmares, depression, an increase in anxiety, and flu-like symptoms. Fortunately, even though I stupidly went cold turkey, I didn't experience the syndrome, perhaps because I had been on a relatively low dose of medication.

But going off medication also sometimes leads to an immediate relapse of OCD symptoms, and this is what happened to me. It's hard to know how an OCD sufferer will react without meds: in general, the more gradually you taper off the medication, the more work you've put into behavior therapy, and the less stressful your life is at the time you quit, the better you'll do.

Even though I had worked hard on my behavior therapy, I was not immune to a relapse. During the move to our new house, our whole life was in boxes and in storage. There is something about living out of boxes that sets my teeth on edge. I was overwhelmed: it would be months before we had everything in its place. Everything was in disarray. I despaired; it had taken five years to get our last house "in shape."

In the midst of this, I started to obsess on the death of my mother-in-law, Matica. When I first started dating Alice, I was a skinny kid. Every time I'd go to the house to pick up Alice, Matica would have a big steak ready for me. She couldn't feed me enough. She doted on me, the exact opposite of Alice's father, Alberto, who once chased me around the house, shouting that I was not good enough for his only daughter.

After we were married, Matica made sure Alice and I had

enough money to live on. She gave us money to landscape the first house we bought—a loan which she never let us repay. Later in her life, after Alberto died, Alice and I looked after her.

I gave the eulogy, my first, at Matica's funeral. I talked about how she had survived the concentration camps of Dachau and Auschwitz. How she had sent me special care packages of Kudalakia, a biscuit-like cookie, when I was living in New York City. How she was the sweetest, most incredible person.

Months later, as painters, plumbers, and carpenters ripped our new house apart, I found myself repeating the eulogy I had delivered over and over again in my mind. It looped through my consciousness. It was clearly an intrusive, obsessive thought, but I didn't identify it as such. I thought I was mourning a wonderful woman whom I had loved.

It didn't occur to me that my OCD might be coming back until one night, nearly dead from moving-induced exhaustion, I decided to cease and desist carrying boxes from the car into the house. I felt slightly uneasy: I couldn't put the car in the garage, which was full of unpacked boxes. In the best of circumstances, I don't like to leave our cars in the driveway; at night, cars belong in the garage. A nice clean driveway makes me feel good. But on this particular night I realized my uneasiness was amplified, although I wasn't sure why. I activated the Toyota's car alarm and went into the house, intending to go straight upstairs to bed.

As soon as I entered the house, though, I felt the old familiar gnawing anxiety. I rushed back outside and checked that the car was actually locked, which, of course, it was. When I reentered the house, the same anxiety came back in full force. That night I went out and checked and rechecked the locks on the car five or six times.

Why am I doing this? I wondered. Calabasas is not the South Bronx. It's a gated community, tightly patrolled by a security force, and crime is nearly nonexistent. My car was in the driveway: even if I'd put out a giant neon sign with big arrows pointing at it that said "Come steal this stuff!" no one would have touched it.

At first, I tried to deny that this was the beginning of a relapse. It was like trying to convince yourself, when you have a sore throat and your body aches, that you're not getting sick. By not recognizing the symptoms for what they are, you think they will go away, but the next morning you have a fever of 102. That's what happened to me. Even as I slid into my relapse, I was up to my old tricks. I would surreptitiously straighten the mirrors, paintings, and glasses in the kitchen cabinet. But I kept it quiet, hidden from my wife and children. I found that I was angry all the time. Angry that the house was in a shambles and my mother-in-law had died and my son was off at college.

I began to lapse into my old state of mind, a state of simmering anxiety, impatience, and anger. I was back at square one, forgetting all the lessons I'd learned from a year and a half on medication and all the hard work I'd done in behavior therapy.

When I went off medication, I tried in vain to recapture the jubilation I had felt when I first went on Luvox and started therapy. Under medication, I had quickly come to feel that my constant anxieties and compulsions no longer controlled me. I'd seen another reality, another way to be. A friend of mine with OCD, a teenager I'll call Gina, describes this shift or transformation as "getting the gorilla of OCD" off her back.

Gina's symptoms were particularly bizarre. She felt overly protective of her younger sister, even felt that she actually controlled her sister's destiny. Whenever her younger sister coughed, sniffled, or sneezed, Gina had to make a specific sound, *baa!*, like a sheep, to ensure nothing bad would happen to the sister. Cough. *Baa!* Cough. *Baa!* The younger sister grew to detest that noise: it drove her into fits of rage. Yet Gina was convinced that if she didn't make the noise something terrible would befall her sister. This created ongoing battles and crazy tension in Gina's household. Imagine yourself as a parent trying to mediate this particular conflict. After Gina started on medication, she improved. The gorilla of her OCD began to loosen its grip.

Another friend of mine, whom I'll call Karen, described a similar feeling when she started treatment for her OCD. Karen is a highly successful conductor of orchestras and choruses. Like me, her OCD has probably helped her in her professional career, by giving her ambition and drive and the perfectionism necessary to be a first-rate musician.

Karen's gorilla had intense checking compulsions. It was convinced that every time she hit a bump in the road, she had run someone over. Whenever she hit a bump, she had to get out of the car and check and recheck that no one was dead on the pavement.

It was moving for me to learn that Karen had OCD, because we had been friends for years, and OCD had hurt our friendship. Before she told me she had the disorder, I hadn't known it. When Alice and I had had Karen and her husband over for dinner they'd often been late—40 minutes, an hour, even more. Well, you know how I react to lateness: I went ballistic. Finally, I asked

Alice to terminate the friendship, because I couldn't stand Karen's lack of punctuality. Then Karen saw me on *Oprah* and called immediately to tell me that she, too, suffered from OCD. That's why she had been late all those years: she couldn't drive the short distance from her house to our house without checking umpteen times whether she had killed someone. Karen has tried medication and behavior therapy for her disorder, but they haven't worked. The gorilla is still there, riding her. Now that I know she suffers from OCD, we're close again.

When I went off medication, I thought my gorilla was gone for good. And I still didn't acknowledge, in the early days of my relapse, that it had come sidling back and had taken its habitual perch, looking over my shoulder, whispering in my ear.

After my checking episode with the locks on the car doors, an incident occurred that made me recognize just how far gone I was. Meredith has a friend who I'll call Jill. She's a great kid: sweet, funny, with an open, trusting personality. Whenever she comes into the house she makes me smile.

I grew up in a house where my parents would always say, "Keep your hands off the walls!" I passed that rule down: my kids and their friends, Jill included, know about my obsession with clean walls, and they're generally careful and cooperative.

Jill came over one night soon after we moved into the house. She's a tall girl, and as she was leaving after visiting Meredith, about 10:00, she slung her daypack over her shoulder. The pack hit the wall, which was freshly painted, and left a thick black streak.

Jill left, oblivious to the horrendous black mark, and to the frustration rising inside me. As soon as she was out the door, I rushed to wash the streak out with a rag, soap, and warm water. "Out, out damn spot!" Nothing doing. There it was, plain as day. I knew what I had to do. Not a moment to lose. I went to the garage. Found the ladder. Found the paint. Found the paint brush. Stirred the paint and put two coats over the mark. Put the paint back on the shelf. Washed out the paintbrush. The whole procedure took over an hour. "Why hadn't I been able to wait at least until morning?" I thought, standing there over the sink in the laundry room, washing the last bit of white latex paint from the brush. I felt ashamed.

Fortunately, I snapped out of my relapse. Our house got back into shape, and life assumed a semblance of order. I felt much less stressed.

I've had other relapses since then, and now I can predict when they'll happen. I'll be overloaded, spread too thin, trying to satisfy everybody. That's what happens to other OCD sufferers I know: they become overwhelmed with their need to be perfect, to return every phone call, to always show up on time, to keep their homes clean. They become exhausted and strung out. I think it's important for all of us to consciously refuse to let ourselves be pulled in twenty directions at once.

New action on the work front also helped snap me out of my first relapse. An old friend, Michael Young, went out of town and asked me to fill in as host for him on *Great Day America,* an afternoon talk show on PAX TV, which is a cable network owned by Bud Paxson, the man who had created the idea of home shopping on television and made millions from it. I took to the show like a fish to water, and when Michael got back into town he asked me to take over as host. He wanted to spend time growing Alton Entertainment, the business he runs which developed *Great Day America* and a number of other shows. Michael also brought me on as Alton's vice president in charge of development.

Since we've been working together, Michael and I have had to realistically assess what's happening in the industry. It's totally different than when I got into the business in '73: the years of risk-taking are gone. It's impossible to put a show on the air just because you believe in it, and then give it time to grow. *Hill Street Blues* and *The Dick Van Dyke Show* were at the bottom of the Nielsen ratings when they were first broadcast. But the heads of the networks on which those shows were broadcast, Fred Silverman at CBS and Brandon Tartikoff at NBC, were both visionaries. When they had a gut feeling about a show they went with it. Now nobody has those kinds of gut feelings—or they're scared to act on them. The industry today is all about dollars and cents. You'd better hope you grab an audience by the throat right away or you're going to be out on the street looking for work. You're always dealing from a position of fear.

On top of this, television is now being aimed at a teen audience. When you're in your forties, like I am, and most shows are geared to fifteen-year-olds, you begin to say, "Wait a second, what am I doing?" I've done warm-ups, I've been the Great MIRAHCFU, I hosted *Double Dare* for years, I did serious news with *Our Home,* and Sissy and I did live talk from New York. You'd think that I'd be content with my success. But television is almost like a drug to me, and I'm not happy unless I'm on camera and performing. It's not something I have a choice about.

I've accepted my role as a daytime television personality. I wouldn't do a nighttime talk show. I'm just not made for it. I don't have the sarcasm, the acerbic wit, and I'm not exceptionally clever—things nighttime guys like Leno, Letterman, and Carson need. Hipper, cooler people are better at night. During the day people want me in their houses. They trust me.

Hosting *Great Day America,* I have the live, informational, news-you-can-use kind of show I do best. We lead off with a celebrity like Ed McMahon, Alan Thicke, or magician Lance Burton. Or we do informational stories on women's health or financial information women can use. I help produce the show and sometimes pick the talent.

But I still haven't attained my goal of hosting a network show that focuses on serious news. I recently came close, but, would you believe it, it was the stigma and ignorance that still surround OCD that kept me from being hired.

I can't mention the name of the show or the personalities involved, but, take it from me, it was a plum of a show, a network job, and I would have been perfect for it. I sent in my tapes, several of the producers loved them, and the show was ready to begin serious discussions about hiring me. Then a powerful executive nixed me because she knew I had OCD. She refused to work with me because she said I would have inflexible perfectionism. If the sound was bad, she said, I wouldn't let the segment run. I'd make them do one shot over and over. It was reported to me that she said, "You can't work with those people," meaning people with OCD.

I suppose I could have sued, but that would have been the end of my career. And one thing I know about this business: people move on. When that executive is gone I'll go to the well again.

Who knows what will happen next time? "The harder you work, the luckier you get" has been my motto.

But, whatever happens, it's been a great ride. If it doesn't get any better than this, I'll die a happy man.

I've had to accept that relapses are a normal part of the disorder. Depending on what's happening in my life I become vulnerable. I've had to learn to say no to people, and to avoid scheduling so many meetings and conference calls one on top of the other. To not be constantly traveling. But even if I have to experience two or three relapses a year, I'd rather be off medication than be relapse-free. That's the life I've chosen for myself. It's an intuitive choice that feels right for me, but it may not be for you. There's nothing wrong with being on medication if that's what feels right. It's a personal decision. If it comes to the point where I feel I'm being overwhelmed by the disorder, I won't hesitate to go back on medication, and I couldn't have gotten where I am now without it. But I think I would need to experience a fairly steady parade of OCD symptoms to start taking the pills again.

I'm immensely grateful for all the medical research that has been done on OCD. Because of many doctors and scientists, I don't obsessively need to fluff the pillows on my couch. I can leave the house with the bed unmade. I can walk down Madison Avenue, see a sign, have an urge to start reading it, and say "Stop it!" to myself. At moments like these, I remember Dr. Hollander's words: "How important do you really think you are? What's your fear? Are you really afraid the plane is going to crash because you haven't read something perfectly?"

And my answer to the last question would always be: "No, I don't really think that."

I'm learning to deal with kids' backpacks banging into walls. Before I was treated for OCD, I would never worry about the child or the child's feelings, just about the wall. Now when a kid scuffs something in the house or stains a carpet I just let it happen. I figure I'll deal with it later, after the kid has gone. I'm conscious of the feelings of others. I don't want to embarrass my own children, and I don't want them or their friends to feel inhibited in my house.

People with OCD have a hard time compromising and putting the needs of others before their own needs. The disorder makes you selfish—your mission is to get rid of your intense feelings of anxiety, and you have to take immediate action. It's hard to worry about anyone who's in the way. Take my friend Karen, for example. She knew I was fuming waiting for her to arrive, but my feelings took a distant second place to her need to stop the car and make sure she hadn't run someone over. One of the greatest side benefits of waging war against OCD and winning is an awakened empathy for others. It's a wonderful feeling to be connected to the rest of humanity instead of being consumed by my own needs.

And it's been an enormous relief to understand that the success of those I love isn't bound up in my rituals. I no longer think the outcome of Meredith's audition for the school play hinges on the fluidity with which I read a sign. In fact, she just got the lead in her high school play, *Once Upon a Mattress,* without my doing one superstitious thing to help her. She doesn't need my help!

OCD has been a shadow lurking in the corners of my life. It wasn't something I enjoyed having, but in some ways it has helped me. It has had a positive side.

It's a great feeling to have faced and overcome OCD. People

who have fought back from a life-threatening illness often feel a special glory in being alive. People who conquer OCD often feel a special kind of freedom or liberation from the obsessions and compulsions that have driven them for years.

Too often we plod through our lives, figuring, "This is just the way I am, this is the way I'll always be." Well, waging war against OCD gives us a chance to step back, take stock of our lives, and make changes. If my story has encouraged one person to gather the courage to get help or feel more confident living with OCD, it will have been worth the telling.

My wife and kids have seen the change in me—that I'm better. But there are still things I'm working on. I want people to walk into our house and feel comfortable, but I'm still uptight, and it gnaws at me. I still get antsy when there are little children in the house; I think they're going to put their hands on the walls, or toddle around with a mouth full of cookies, dribbling crumbs on the floor. And I'm still waiting for the day when I'll be able to say to Meredith, "Why don't you invite fifty of your friends over for a party?" That's my goal: to feel comfortable with fifty teenagers partying hard late into the night in our house, leaning against the walls, dancing on the carpets, their jackets tossed hither and yon, bowls of chips knocked over on the living room floor, glasses spilled, glasses broken, chaos and mayhem, everything out of place.

| *epilogue* |

Since the publication of this book in October of 1999, my life has been changed in many ways. I have noticed how three simple letters, OCD, have become more mainstream, not only in the media, but amongst the general public as well. This did not happen overnight. Over the past four years in my travels crossing the country, first with a campaign based on awareness with children and currently focusing on adults coping, it seemed that my time was spent mostly explaining the basics of the disorder . . . over and over again.

Now, it has almost become the "hip" disorder! Several times recently, talk show goddess Rosie O'Donnell referred to her life and perhaps her "OCD" kicking in. Does she really have it . . . who knows? But my point is, when she or someone else mutters the words "obsessive compulsive disorder," almost nobody questions what it is.

I have noticed that when people attend my speaking engagements, they come better prepared, asking hard-hitting, in-your-face-type questions. They are there because they are seeking answers, in public, with less and less stigma attached. For this I am truly grateful.

While out promoting the book, I was able to spend many hours doing talk radio. In the process, I had an amazing opportunity to speak one-on-one with individuals who either have OCD or know someone who does. Each story is truly unique, and yet the similarities remain the same. These people are usually highly intelligent, know that their actions are generally irrational, and want to stop, yet either need more information on where to get help, or that extra push to begin behavior modification and in some cases, medication. They have told me that because of my voice, OCD now has a face and they are moved to, at least, speak more freely on the topic. It is all about helping others, and I truly understand and applaud the actions of someone like Michael J. Fox, putting a face on Parkinson's, taking away some of the fear and stigma attached to that medical condition.

Inside Edition did a piece on the book that also featured Howard Stern, Roseanne, and Howie Mandel as well as myself. The reaction was that many now feel more at ease to discuss their own stories and are also impressed by the amount of people who have obsessive compulsive disorder and are able to not only overcome it, but also become successful in their chosen line of work. When I appeared on ABC television's, *The View* with Barbara Walters, co-host Lisa Ling discussed, openly on the air, her feelings as to why she felt she might have OCD. Once again, another successful person, in the public eye, not ashamed to tell her story.

As for my career, I have jumped back and forth, producing sometimes and, more recently, moving back in front of the camera. My producing chores included a show for the Fox Family channel,

I Can't Believe You Said That, starring NBA player John Salley, and then I created and executive produced a program for The Health Channel called *The Parent Table*. I recently completed a pilot for The History Channel called *History IQ* that was sold and begins airing in October every weeknight, as well as hosted a new series for the Food Network called *It's a Surprise*. But believe it or not, Nickelodeon and Double Dare and the world of slime have creeped back into my life!

In Chapter 6, "Earthquake," I mentioned that although hosting *Double Dare* again had little interest to me, producing a new version did. Well, this past January I got my wish! As Consulting Producer of *Double Dare 2000*, I was able to take the program to the next level and yes, even got slimed again . . . twice! Once for a promo tape seen only by television critics across the country, but also on a special called *SNICK House*, where I had my farewell sliming. And you know what? I actually enjoyed it . . . for two reasons. The first being that it marked another transition in my show business career, but more importantly, because it proved to me, personally, once and for all, that not only have I been able to help others, but in the process, help myself. It was a great feeling.

resource guide

Anxiety Disorders Association of America
11900 Parklawn Drive, Suite 100
Rockville, MD 20852-2624
(301) 231-9350
www.adaa.org

Freedom from Fear
308 Seaview Avenue
Staten Island, NY 10305
(718) 351-1717
www.freedomfromfear.com

National Alliance for the Mentally Ill (NAMI)
200 North Glebe Road, Suite 1015
Arlington, VA 22203-3754
(800) 950-6264
www.nami.org

National Institute of Mental Health
c/o Information Resources and Inquiries
5600 Fishers Lane, Room 7C-02
Rockville, MD 20857
(301) 443-4513
(888) 826-9438 (publications)
www.nimh.gov

National Mental Health Association
1021 Prince Street
Alexandria, VA 22314-2971
(703) 684-7722
www.nmha.org

National OCD Resource Center*
(800) NEWS-4-OCD
(800) 639-7462
OCD Resource Center Website
http://www.ocdresource.com
*Presented by Solvay Pharmaceuticals, Inc., and Pharmacia &
Upjohn

Obsessive Compulsive Foundation
P.O. Box 70
Milford, CT 06460
(203) 878-5669
www.ocfoundation.org

about the author

Marc Summers is the former host of Nickelodeon's popular *Double Dare* game show, ABC's *Home Show*, Lifetime's *Our Home*, and PAX TV's *Great Day America*. As a national spokesperson for the Obsessive Compulsive Foundation, he has appeared on *Oprah*, *Today*, *Dateline*, and the *Howard Stern Show*, and has been profiled in *People* and *USA Today*. Summers lives in Los Angeles. **Eric Hollander, M.D.**, is professor of psychiatry, director of clinical psychopharmacology, director of the Compulsive, Impulsive, and Anxiety Disorders Program, and clinical director of the Seaver Autism Research Center at Mount Sinai School of Medicine. Marc's collaborators on this book are **Kenneth Wapner** and **Jennifer Wolfson**, who run Peekamoose Productions in Woodstock, New York, a company involved in developing, writing, and editing books.